# curries

### essential recipes

**Publisher's Note:**
Raw or semi-cooked eggs should not be consumed by babies, toddlers, pregnant women,
the elderly or those suffering from recurring illness.

**Recipe Note:**
All eggs and vegetables are medium sized, unless otherwise stated.

Publisher and Creative Director: Nick Wells
Project Editor: Cat Emslie
Copy Editor: Kathy Steer
Photographers: Colin Bowling, Paul Forrester and Stephen Brayne
Home Economists & Stylists: Ann Nicol, Jaqueline Bellefontaine,
Mandy Phipps, Vicki Smallwood and Penny Stephens
Art Director: Mike Spender
Layout Design: Dave Jones
Digital Design and Production: Chris Herbert and Claire Walker
Proofreader: Dawn Laker

12 11

5 7 9 10 8 6

This edition first published 2008 by
**FLAME TREE PUBLISHING**
Crabtree Hall, Crabtree Lane
Fulham, London SW6 6TY
United Kingdom

www.flametreepublishing.com

Flame Tree is part of the Foundry Creative Media Co. Ltd

© 2008 this edition The Foundry Creative Media Co. Ltd

ISBN 978-1-84786-997-5

A CIP record for this book is available from the British Library upon request.

Printed in China

# curries

## essential recipes

General Editor: Gina Steer

**FLAME TREE
PUBLISHING**

# Contents

## Fish & Seafood

## Vegetables

# Hygiene in the Kitchen

It is important to remember that many foods can carry some form of bacteria. In most cases, the worst it will lead to is a bout of food poisoning or gastroenteritis, although for certain people this can be serious. The risk can be reduced or eliminated, however, by good hygiene and proper cooking.

Do not buy food that is past its sell-by date and do not consume food that is past its use-by date. When buying food, use the eyes and nose. If the food looks tired, limp or a bad colour or it has a rank, acrid or simply bad smell, do not buy or eat it under any circumstances.

Dish cloths and tea towels must be washed and changed regularly. Ideally use disposable cloths and replace on a daily basis. More durable cloths should be left to soak in bleach, then washed in the washing machine at a high temperature. Keep hands, utensils and food preparation surfaces clean and do not allow pets to climb onto work surfaces. Avoid handling food if suffering from an upset stomach as bacteria can be passed on through food preparation.

## Buying

Avoid bulk buying where possible, especially fresh produce. Fresh foods lose their nutritional value rapidly, so buying a little at a time minimises loss of nutrients. Check that any packaging is intact and not damaged or pierced at all. Store fresh foods in the refrigerator as soon as possible.

When buying frozen foods, ensure that they are not heavily iced on the outside and that the contents feel completely frozen. Ensure that they have been stored in the cabinet at the correct storage level and the temperature is below -18°C/-0.4°F. Pack in cool bags to transport home and place in the freezer as soon as possible after purchase.

## Preparation

Take special care when preparing raw meat and fish. Separate chopping boards should be used for each, and the knife, board and your hands should be thoroughly washed before handling or preparing any other food. Good quality plastic boards are available in various designs and colours. This makes differentiating easier and the plastic has the added hygienic advantage of being washable at high temperatures in the dishwasher. If using the board for fish, first wash in cold water, then in hot to prevent odour.

When cooking, be particularly careful to keep cooked and raw food separate to avoid any contamination. It is worth washing all fruits and vegetables regardless of whether they are going to be eaten raw or lightly cooked. This rule should apply even to prewashed herbs and salads.

Do not reheat food more than once. If using a microwave, always check that the food is piping hot all the way through – in theory, the food should reach 70°C/158°F and needs to be cooked at that temperature for at least three minutes to ensure that all bacteria are killed.

All poultry must be thoroughly thawed before using. Remove the food to be thawed from the freezer and place in a shallow dish to contain the juices. Leave the food in the refrigerator until it is completely thawed. A 1.4 kg/3 lb whole chicken will take about 26–30 hours to thaw. To speed up the process, immerse the chicken in cold water, making sure that the water is changed regularly. When the joints can move freely and no ice crystals remain in the cavity, the bird is completely thawed. Once thawed, remove the wrapper and pat dry. Place the chicken in a shallow dish, cover lightly

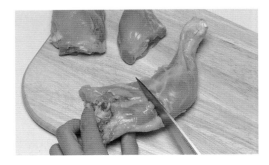

and store as close to the base of the refrigerator as possible. The chicken should be cooked as soon as possible.

Some foods can be cooked from frozen including many prepacked foods such as soups, sauces, casseroles and breads. Where applicable follow the manufacturers' instructions. Vegetables and fruits can also be cooked from frozen, but meats and fish should be thawed first. The only time food can be refrozen is when the food has been thoroughly thawed then cooked. Once the food has cooled then it can be frozen again, but it should only be stored for one month.

All poultry and game (except for duck) must be cooked thoroughly. When cooked, the juices will run clear on the thickest part of the bird – the best area to try is usually the thigh. Other meats, like beef, lamb and pork should be cooked right the way through. Fish should turn opaque, be firm in texture and break easily into large flakes.

Make sure leftovers are reheated until piping hot and that any sauce or soup reaches boiling point first.

## Storing, Refrigerating and Freezing

Meat, poultry, fish, seafood and dairy products should all be refrigerated. The temperature of the refrigerator should be between 1–5°C/34–41°F, while the freezer temperature should not rise above -18°C/-0.4°F. To ensure the optimum temperature, avoid leaving the door open for long periods. Try not to overstock as this reduces the airflow inside and therefore the effectiveness in cooling the food within.

When refrigerating cooked food, allow it to cool down quickly and completely before refrigerating. Hot food will raise the temperature of the refrigerator and possibly affect or spoil other food stored in it.

Food should always be covered. Raw and cooked food should be stored in separate parts of the refrigerator. Cooked food should be kept on the top shelves, while raw meat, poultry and fish should be placed on the bottom to avoid drips and cross-contamination. It is recommended that eggs be refrigerated in order to maintain their freshness and shelf life.

Regularly clean, defrost and clear out the refrigerator and freezer – it is worth checking the packaging to see exactly how long each product is safe to freeze. Take care that frozen foods are not stored in the freezer for too long. Blanched vegetables can be stored for one month; beef, lamb, poultry and pork for six months and unblanched vegetables and fruits in syrup for a year. Oily fish and sausages should be stored for three months. Dairy products can last four to six months, while cakes and pastries can be kept in the freezer for three to six months.

## High Risk Foods

Certain foods may carry risks to people who are considered vulnerable such as the elderly, the ill, pregnant women, babies, young infants and those suffering from a recurring illness.

There is a slight chance that some eggs carry the bacteria salmonella. Cook the eggs until both the yolk and the white are firm to eliminate this risk. Pay particular attention to dishes and products incorporating lightly cooked or raw eggs, such as hollandaise sauce, mayonnaise, mousses, soufflés, meringues, custard-based dishes, ice creams and sorbets. Certain meats and poultry also carry the potential risk of salmonella and so should be cooked thoroughly until the juices run clear and there is no pinkness left. Unpasteurised products such as milk, cheese (especially soft cheese), pâté, meat (raw and cooked) all have the potential risk of listeria and should be avoided.

When buying seafood, buy from a reputable source which has a high turnover to ensure freshness. Fish should have bright clear eyes, shiny skin and bright pink or red gills. The fish should feel stiff to the touch, with a slight smell of sea air and iodine. The flesh of fish steaks and fillets should be translucent with no signs of discolouration. Molluscs such as scallops and mussels are sold fresh and are still alive. Avoid any that are open or do not close when tapped lightly, also discard any that do not open after cooking. In the same way, univalves such as cockles or winkles should withdraw back into their shells when lightly prodded. When choosing cephalopods such as squid and octopus they should have a firm flesh and pleasant sea smell.

As with all fish, whether it is shellfish or seafish, care is required when freezing it. It is imperative to check whether the fish has been frozen before. If it has been frozen, then it should not be frozen again under any circumstances.

# Nutrition: The Role of Essential Nutrients

A healthy and well-balanced diet is the body's primary energy source. In children, it constitutes the building blocks for future health as well as providing lots of energy. In adults, it encourages self-healing and regeneration within the body. A well-balanced diet will provide the body with all the essential nutrients it needs. This can be achieved by eating a variety of foods, demonstrated in the pyramid below.

## FATS

### PROTEINS

milk, yogurt      meat, fish, poultry,
and cheese      eggs, nuts and pulses

### FRUITS AND VEGETABLES

### STARCHY CARBOHYDRATES

cereals, potatoes, bread, rice and pasta

## FATS

Fats fall into two categories: saturated and unsaturated. Fats are an essential part of the diet as they are a source of energy and provide essential fatty acids and fat-soluble vitamins, but it is very important that a healthy balance is achieved. The right balance should boost the body's immunity to infection and keep muscles, nerves and arteries in good condition. Saturated fats are of animal origin and can be found in dairy produce, meat, eggs, margarines and hard white cooking fat (lard) as well as in manufactured products such as pies, biscuits and cakes. A high intake of saturated fat over many years has been proven to increase heart disease and high blood cholesterol levels and often leads to weight gain. Lowering the amount of saturated fat that we consume is very important, but this does not mean that it is good to consume lots of other types of fat.

There are two kinds of unsaturated fats: polyunsaturated and monounsaturated. Polyunsaturated fats include safflower, soybean, corn and sesame oils. The Omega-3 oils in polyunsaturated fats have been found to be beneficial to coronary health and can encourage brain growth and development. They are derived from oily fish such as salmon, mackerel, herring, pilchards and sardines. It is recommended that we should eat these types of fish at least once a week. Alternative liver oil supplements are also available. The most popular oils that are high in monounsaturates are olive oil, sunflower oil and peanut oil. Monounsaturated fats are also known to help reduce the levels of cholesterol.

## PROTEINS

Composed of amino acids – proteins' building blocks – proteins perform a wide variety of essential functions for the body, including supplying energy and building and repairing tissues. Good sources of proteins are eggs, milk, yogurt, cheese, meat, fish, poultry, nuts and pulses. (See the second level of the pyramid.) Some of these foods, however, contain saturated fats. To strike a nutritional balance, eat generous amounts of vegetable protein foods such as soya, beans, lentils, peas and nuts.

# MINERALS

**CALCIUM** Important for healthy bones and teeth, nerve transmission, muscle contraction, blood clotting and hormone function. Also promotes a healthy heart and skin, relieves aching muscles and bones, maintains the correct acid-alkaline balance and reduces menstrual cramps. Good sources are dairy products, small bones of small fish, nuts, pulses, fortified white flours, breads and green leafy vegetables.

**CHROMIUM** Chromium balances blood sugar levels, helps to reduce cravings, improves lifespan, helps protect DNA and is essential for heart function. Good sources are brewer's yeast, wholemeal bread, rye bread, oysters, potatoes, green peppers, butter and parsnips.

**IODINE** Important for the manufacture of thyroid hormones and for normal development. Good sources are seafood, seaweed, milk and dairy.

**IRON** As a component of haemoglobin, iron carries oxygen around the body. It is vital for normal growth and development. Good sources are liver, corned beef, red meat, fortified breakfast cereals, pulses, green leafy vegetables, egg yolk, cocoa and cocoa products.

**MAGNESIUM** Important for efficient functioning of metabolic enzymes and development of the skeleton. Magnesium promotes healthy muscles by helping them to relax and is therefore good for PMS. It is also important for heart muscles and the nervous system. Good sources are nuts, green vegetables, meat, cereals, milk and yogurt.

**PHOSPHORUS** Forms and maintains bones and teeth, builds muscle tissue, helps maintain pH of the body and aids metabolism and energy production. Phosphorus is present in almost all foods.

**POTASSIUM** Enables processing of nutrients; promotes healthy nerves and muscles; maintains fluid balance; helps secretion of insulin for blood sugar control; relaxes muscles; maintains heart functioning and stimulates gut movement. Good sources are fruit, vegetables, milk and bread.

**SELENIUM** Antioxidant properties help to protect against free radicals and carcinogens. Selenium reduces inflammation, stimulates the immune system, promotes a healthy heart and helps vitamin E's action. Necessary for the male reproductive system and for metabolism. Good sources are tuna, liver, kidney, meat, eggs, cereals, nuts and dairy products.

**SODIUM** Important in helping to control body fluid, preventing dehydration. Sodium is involved in muscle and nerve function and helps move nutrients into cells. All foods are good sources. Processed, pickled and salted foods are richest in sodium but should be eaten in moderation.

**ZINC** Important for metabolism and healing; aids ability to cope with stress; promotes a healthy nervous system and brain, especially in the growing foetus; aids bone and teeth formation and is essential for energy. Good sources are liver, meat, pulses, whole-grain cereals, nuts and oysters.

# VITAMINS

**VITAMIN A** Important for cell growth and development and for the formation of visual pigments in the eye. Vitamin A comes in two forms: retinol and beta-carotens. Retinol is found in liver, meat and whole milk. Beta-carotene is a powerful antioxidant and is found in red and yellow fruits and vegetables such as carrots, mangoes and apricots.

**VITAMIN B1** Important in releasing energy from carbohydrate-containing foods. Good sources are yeast and yeast products, bread, fortified breakfast cereals and potatoes.

**VITAMIN B2** Important for metabolism of proteins, fats and carbohydrates to produce energy. Good sources are meat, yeast extracts, fortified breakfast cereals and milk and its products.

**VITAMIN B3** Required for the metabolism of food into energy. Good sources are milk, fortified cereals, pulses, meat, poultry and eggs.

**VITAMIN B5** Important for the metabolism of food and energy production. All foods are good sources but especially fortified breakfast cereals, whole-grain bread and dairy products.

**VITAMIN B6** Important for metabolism of protein and fat. Vitamin B6 may also be involved in the regulation of sex hormones. Good sources are liver, fish, pork, soya beans and peanuts.

**VITAMIN B12** Important for the production of red blood cells and DNA. It is vital for growth and the nervous system. Good sources are meat, fish, eggs, poultry and milk.

**BIOTIN** Important for metabolism of fatty acids. Good sources of biotin are liver, kidney, eggs and nuts.

**VITAMIN C** Important for healing wounds and the formation of collagen which keeps skin and bones strong. It is an important antioxidant. Good sources are fruits, especially soft summer fruits, and vegetables.

**VITAMIN D** Important for absorption and handling of calcium to help build bone strength. Good sources are oily fish, eggs, whole milk and milk products, margarine and of course sufficient exposure to sunlight, as vitamin D is made in the skin.

**VITAMIN E** Important as an antioxidant vitamin helping to protect cell membranes from damage. Good sources are vegetable oils, margarines, seeds, nuts and green vegetables.

**FOLIC ACID** Critical during pregnancy for the development of the brain and nerves. It is always essential for brain and nerve function and is needed for utilising protein and red blood cell formation. Good sources are whole-grain cereals, fortified cereals, green leafy vegetables, oranges and liver.

**VITAMIN K** Important for controlling blood clotting. Good sources are cauliflower, Brussels sprouts, lettuce, cabbage, beans, broccoli, peas, asparagus, potatoes, corn oil, tomatoes and milk.

# CARBOHYDRATES

Carbohydrates are an energy source and come in two forms: starch and sugar. Starch carbohydrates are also known as complex carbohydrates and they include all cereals, potatoes, breads, rice and pasta. Eating whole-grain varieties of these foods also provides fibre. Diets high in fibre are believed to be beneficial in helping to prevent bowel cancer and keep cholesterol down. Sugar carbohydrates – also known as fast-release because they provide a quick fix of energy – include sugar and sugar-sweetened products. Other sugars are lactose (from milk) and fructose (from fruit).

# Meat

Bored of bland beef and lacking lamb? Cook up a curry and give your dinner the kick it needs! Flavours and spices abound in such dishes as Malaysian Beef Satay and Lamb Passanda. These recipes don't sound exotic enough to drive away the dinner doldrums? Then Kashmir Kid or Roghan Josh are must-tries to enliven your evening.

# Thai Beef Curry with Lemon & Basmati Rice

**1** Trim the beef fillet, discarding any fat, then cut across the grain into thin slices. Heat a wok, add the oil and, when hot, add the green curry paste and cook for 30 seconds. Add the beef strips and stir-fry for 3–4 minutes.

**2** Add the pepper strips and the celery and continue to stir-fry for 2 minutes. Add the lemon juice, Thai fish sauce and sugar and cook for a further 3–4 minutes, or until the beef is tender and cooked to personal preference.

**3** Meanwhile, cook the rice in a saucepan of lightly salted boiling water for 10–12 minutes, or until tender. Drain, rinse with boiling water and drain again. Return to the saucepan and add the butter. Cover and allow the butter to melt before spooning onto a large serving dish. Sprinkle the cooked curry with the chopped coriander and serve immediately with the rice and crème fraîche.

## Ingredients    SERVES 4

450 g/1 lb beef fillet
1 tbsp groundnut or vegetable oil
2 tbsp Thai green curry paste
1 green pepper, deseeded, cut into strips
1 red pepper, deseeded and cut
   into strips
1 celery stick, trimmed and sliced
juice of 1 fresh lemon
2 tsp Thai fish sauce
2 tsp demerara sugar
225 g/8 oz basmati rice
15 g/$^1/_2$ oz butter
2 tbsp freshly chopped coriander
4 tbsp crème fraîche

### Tasty tip

To make green curry paste, finely chop together 3–4 deseeded hot green chillies, 1 lemon grass stalk, 2 shallots, 3 garlic cloves, small piece galangal or ginger, 1 teaspoon ground coriander, $^1/_2$ teaspoon ground cumin, 2 kaffir lime leaves and a handful of fresh coriander. Refrigerate for up to 1 month.

# Beef & Mushroom Curry

1. Put the steak between two sheets of baking paper then place on a chopping board. Beat with either a meat mallet or rolling pin until flattened then trim off and discard the fat and cut into thin strips. Heat the oil in a saucepan, add the beef and fry until sealed, stirring frequently. Remove beef and place to one side.

2. Fry the onions, garlic, ginger, chillies, curry paste and coriander for 2 minutes. Add the mushrooms, stock and tomatoes and season to taste.

3. Return the beef to the pan. Cover the pan and simmer gently for 1¼ – 1½ hours or until the beef is tender.

4. Place the rice in a saucepan of boiling salted water, and simmer for 15 minutes until tender or according to the package instructions. Drain the rice then return to the saucepan, add the butter, cover and keep warm.

5. Stir the creamed coconut and ground almonds into the curry, cover the pan and cook gently for 3 minutes. Serve with the rice.

## Ingredients          SERVES 4

700 g/1½ lb rump steak
3 tbsp vegetable oil
2 onions, peeled and thinly sliced
    into rings
2 garlic cloves, peeled and crushed
2.5 cm/1 inch piece root
    ginger, chopped
2 fresh green chillies, deseeded
    and chopped
1½ tbsp medium curry paste
1 tsp ground coriander
225g/8oz button mushrooms,
    wiped and sliced
900 ml/1½ pints beef stock
3 tomatoes, chopped
salt and freshly ground black pepper
350g/12oz long-grain rice
50g/2oz butter
50g/2oz creamed coconut, chopped
2 tbsp ground almonds

## Helpful hint

Beating the steak breaks down the connective tissue thus making it more tender.

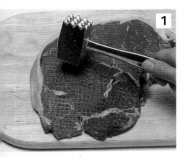

# Goan-style Beef Curry

1 Place the onions, garlic, ginger and spices in a food processor and blend to a paste.

2 Spread half the paste half over the steak, then sprinkle lightly with salt. Leave to marinate in the refrigerator for at least 15 minutes.

3 Cut the beef into small strips. Heat 1 tablespoon of the oil in a heavy-based saucepan, add the beef and fry on all sides for 5 minutes, or until sealed. Remove from the pan and reserve.

4 Add the remaining oil to the pan, then add the halved chillies and fry for 2 minutes. Remove and reserve. Stir the remaining paste into the oil left in the pan and cook for a further 3 minutes. Return the beef to the pan with the beef stock and bring to the boil.

5 Reduce the heat, cover and simmer for 30–40 minutes, or until tender. Garnish with the halved chillies and serve.

## Ingredients  SERVES 4–6

2 onions, peeled and chopped
2–3 garlic cloves, peeled
    and chopped
5 cm/2 inch piece fresh root ginger,
    peeled and grated
1 tsp chilli powder
1 tsp turmeric
1 tsp ground coriander
1 tsp ground cumin
freshly milled salt
450 g/1 lb braising steak, trimmed
2 tbsp vegetable oil
2 green chillies, deseeded and cut in
    half lengthways
2 red chillies, deseeded and cut in
    half lengthways
450 ml/³/₄ pint beef stock

### Food fact
Beef is not eaten in most parts of India as it is forbidden by the Hindu religion.

# Malaysian Beef Curry

1   Soak the wooden skewers in cold water for 30 minutes. Meanwhile, trim the steak, cut into narrow strips and place in a shallow dish.

2   Heat the oil in a small frying pan, add the seeds and fry for 30 seconds, or until they pop. Add the chillies, crushed garlic and curry paste and continue to fry, stirring, for 2 minutes. Remove from the heat and gradually blend in the coconut milk and allow to cool. Pour over the beef, cover lightly and leave to marinate in the refrigerator for at least 30 minutes.

3   When ready to cook, preheat the grill to high and line the grill rack with foil. Drain the skewers and beef, reserving the remaining marinade. Thread the beef strips onto the skewers and place under the preheated grill for 8–10 minutes, or until cooked to personal preference, brushing occasionally with the remaining marinade.

4   Meanwhile, place all the ingredients for the sauce in a small saucepan and heat gently for 3–5 minutes, stirring occasionally.

## Ingredients          SERVES 4–6

450 g/1 lb beef steak,
   such as rump or sirloin
1 tbsp vegetable oil
1 tsp fennel seeds
1 tsp fenugreek seeds
2 red chillies, deseeded and chopped
2 garlic cloves, peeled and crushed
1 tbsp Thai red curry paste
200 ml/7 fl oz coconut milk
8 wooden kebab skewers

### For the satay sauce:

1 small red chilli, deseeded and
   finely chopped
1 tbsp lime juice
50 ml/2 fl oz fish sauce
2 tbsp smooth peanut butter
1 tbsp roasted peanuts, finely chopped
2 spring onions, trimmed and
   finely chopped

### Tasty tip

For a nuttier sauce, replace the smooth peanut butter with the crunchy version.

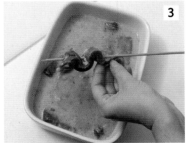

# Vietnamese-style Aromatic Beef

1 Trim the meat, cut into bite-sized chunks and reserve. Heat the oil in a large heavy-based frying pan, add the cardamom pods, cinnamon stick, star anise and lemon grass and gently fry for 2 minutes. Add the chilli and continue to fry for a further 2 minutes.

2 Add the meat to the pan and stir-fry for 5 minutes, or until the meat is sealed.

3 Add the curry paste and the onions and garlic and fry for a further 5 minutes before stirring in the beef stock and coconut milk.

4 Bring to the boil, then reduce the heat, cover and simmer for 1½ hours, stirring occasionally. Add the soy sauce and carrots and continue to cook for a further 30 minutes. Add the sugar snap peas and cook for 10 minutes, or until the meat and vegetables are tender. Remove the cinnamon stick and whole anise and serve.

## Ingredients    SERVES 4–6

550 g/1¼ lb stewing steak
2 tbsp vegetable oil
5 cardamom pods, cracked
1 cinnamon stick, bruised
3 whole star anise
2 lemon grass stalks, outer leaves
    discarded and bruised
1 small green chilli, deseeded
    and chopped
1–2 tbsp medium hot curry paste
2 red onions, peeled and cut
    into wedges
2 garlic cloves, peeled and sliced
450 ml/¾ pint beef stock
150 ml/¼ pint coconut milk
1 tbsp soy sauce
225 g/8 oz carrots, peeled and sliced
175 g/6 oz sugar snap peas

## Tasty tip
For a change, try serving this with freshly cooked noodles.

# Jerked Steaks

1 Blend all the ingredients for the jerk sauce then rub over the steaks. Place on a plate, lightly cover and leave in the refrigerator for at least 30 minutes.

2 Mix together all the ingredients for the mango relish, cover and leave for 30 minutes to allow the flavours to develop.

3 When ready to cook, heat a griddle pan or heavy-based frying pan until hot and a few drops of water sizzle when dropped into the pan. Add the steaks and cook for 2–3 minutes on each side for rare, 3–4 minutes on each side for medium and 5–6 minutes on each side for well done.

4 Remove from the pan and serve with the prepared relish, salad and potato wedges.

## Ingredients     SERVES 4–6

4 rump/sirloin steaks, c. 100 g/4 oz each

### For the jerk sauce:

1 tsp ground allspice; 25 g/1 oz light muscovado sugar; 1–2 garlic cloves, peeled and chopped; 1 small red chilli, deseeded and chopped; few fresh thyme sprigs, leaves removed; 1 tsp ground cinnamon; 1/4 tsp freshly grated nutmeg; salt and freshly ground black pepper; 1 tbsp soy sauce

### For the mango relish:

1 ripe mango, peeled, stoned and finely chopped; 6 spring onions, trimmed and chopped; 1–2 garlic cloves, peeled and crushed; 1 red chilli, deseeded and chopped; 1 small, ripe but firm banana, peeled and chopped; 1 tbsp lime juice; 1 tbsp clear honey, warmed; 50 g/2 oz unsweetened chopped dates; 1 tsp ground cinnamon

### To serve:

salad; potato wedges

# Massaman Beef Curry

1  Trim the beef, cut into thin strips and reserve. Heat 2 tablespoons of the oil in a heavy-based saucepan, add the ginger and chillies and fry for 3 minutes. Add the onions and garlic and continue to fry for 5 minutes, or until the onions have softened.

2  Remove the onions and garlic with a slotted spoon and add the beef to the pan. Cook, stirring, for 5 minutes, or until sealed.

3  Add the curry paste and continue to fry for 3 minutes, then return the onions and garlic to the pan and stir well.

4  Pour the coconut milk and stock into the pan and bring to the boil. Reduce the heat, cover and simmer for 30 minutes, stirring occasionally.

5  Add the potatoes to the pan, with more stock if necessary, then continue to simmer for 20–25 minutes, or until the meat and potatoes are cooked. Meanwhile, heat the remaining oil in a small saucepan, add the green pepper strips and fry for 2 minutes. Add the chopped peanuts and fry for 1 minute, stirring constantly. Sprinkle over the cooked curry and serve.

## Ingredients    SERVES 4–6

450 g/1 lb beef steak, such as sirloin or rump
3 tbsp vegetable oil
5 cm/2 inch piece fresh root ginger, peeled and grated
3 green bird's eye chillies, deseeded and chopped
2 red onions, peeled and chopped
3 garlic cloves, peeled and crushed
2 tbsp Massaman Thai curry paste
400 ml/14 fl oz coconut milk
150–200 ml/5–7 fl oz beef stock
350 g/12 oz new potatoes, scrubbed and cut into small chunks
1 green pepper, deseeded and cut into strips
50 g/2 oz roasted peanuts, chopped

## Helpful hint

If a hotter curry is preferred, increase the number of chillies and add 1 tablespoon of chilli powder when frying the onions and garlic.

# Caribbean Empanadas

1 Place the mince in a nonstick frying pan and cook, stirring, for 5–8 minutes, or until sealed. Break up any lumps with a wooden spoon. Add the onion, chilli and red pepper together with the spices and cook, stirring, for 10 minutes, or until the onion has softened. Sprinkle in the sugar.

2 Blend the tomato purée with the water and stir into the meat. Bring to the boil, then reduce the heat and simmer for 10 minutes. Allow to cool.

3 Roll the pastry out on a lightly floured surface and cut into 10 cm/4 inch rounds. Place a spoonful of the meat mixture onto the centre of each pastry round and brush the edges with water.  Fold over, encasing the filling to form small pasties.

4 Heat the oil to a temperature of 180°C/350°F and deep-fry the empanadas in batches, about 3 or 4 at a time, for 3–4 minutes, or until golden. Drain on absorbent kitchen paper. Garnish and serve with the mango relish.

## Ingredients    SERVES 4–6

175 g/6 oz lean fresh beef mince
175 g/6 oz lean fresh pork mince
1 onion, peeled and finely chopped
1 Scotch bonnet chilli, deseeded and
  finely chopped
1 small red pepper, deseeded and
  finely chopped
$^1/_2$ tsp ground cloves
1 tsp ground cinnamon
$^1/_2$ tsp ground allspice
1 tsp sugar
1 tbsp tomato purée
6 tbsp water
700 g/1$^1/_2$ lb prepared
  shortcrust pastry
vegetable oil, for deep-frying
fresh herbs, to garnish
mango relish (see pages 22 and 180)

### Tasty tip
If preferred, the empanadas can be oven baked. Brush with melted butter then cook in a preheated oven at 200°C/400°F/Gas Mark 6 for 20 minutes.

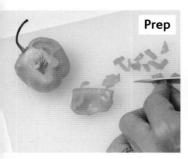
**Prep**

**1**

**3**

# Thai Beef Curry

1 Trim the beef discarding any fat and gristle, cut into bite-sized chunks and reserve. Heat the oil in a heavy-based saucepan, add the chillies, garlic and ginger and fry for 2 minutes. Add the Thai green curry paste and onions and fry for 5 minutes, or until the onion has begun to soften.

2 Add the beef to the pan and continue to fry for a further 5 minutes, or until sealed and lightly coated in the spices.

3 Pour in the lime juice, stock and coconut milk, then add the soy and fish sauces. Stir and add the sugar. Bring to the boil, reduce the heat, cover and simmer, stirring occasionally, for 2 hours, or until the meat is tender. Sprinkle with chopped coriander and serve with freshly cooked noodles.

## Ingredients    SERVES 4–6

550 g/1¼ lb stewing beef
2 tbsp vegetable oil
1–2 bird's eye chillies, deseeded
2–3 garlic cloves, peeled
    and chopped
5 cm/2 inch piece fresh root ginger,
    peeled and grated
2–3 tsp Thai green curry paste,
    or to taste
2 onions, peeled and chopped
2 tbsp lime juice
450 ml/¾ pint beef stock
300 ml/½ pint coconut milk
1 tsp soy sauce
1 tbsp fish sauce
1–2 tsp sugar
2 tbsp freshly chopped coriander
freshly cooked egg noodles, to serve

## Helpful hint

Check the level of liquid during cooking and if it is evaporating too quickly, add some more beef stock and reduce the heat.

# Spicy Lamb in Yogurt Sauce

1  Blend the chilli powder, cinnamon, curry powder, cumin and seasoning with 2 tablespoons of the oil in a bowl and reserve. Cut the lamb fillet into thin strips, add to the spice and oil mixture and stir until coated thoroughly. Cover and leave to marinate in the refrigerator for at least 30 minutes.

2  Heat the wok, then pour in the remaining oil. When hot, add the cardamom pods and cloves and stir-fry for 10 seconds. Add the onion, garlic and ginger to the wok and stir-fry for 3–4 minutes until softened.

3  Add the lamb with the marinade ingredients and stir-fry for a further 3 minutes until cooked. Pour in the yogurt, stir thoroughly and heat until piping hot. Sprinkle with the chopped coriander and sliced spring onions then serve immediately with freshly cooked rice and naan bread.

## Ingredients                SERVES 4

1 tsp hot chilli powder
1 tsp ground cinnamon
1 tsp medium hot curry powder
1 tsp ground cumin
salt and freshly ground black pepper
3 tbsp groundnut oil
450 g/1 lb lamb fillet, trimmed
4 cardamom pods, cracked
4 whole cloves
1 onion, peeled and finely sliced
2 garlic cloves, peeled and crushed
2.5 cm/1 inch piece fresh root ginger, peeled and grated
150 ml/$^{1}/_{4}$ pint Greek-style yogurt
1 tbsp freshly chopped coriander
2 spring onions, trimmed and finely sliced

**To serve:**
freshly cooked rice
naan bread

# Curried Lamb Pilaf

1 Preheat the oven to 140°C/ 275°F/Gas Mark 1. Heat the oil in a flameproof casserole with a tight-fitting lid and add the almonds. Cook for about 1 minute until just starting to brown, stirring often. Add the onion, carrot and celery and cook gently for a further 8–10 minutes until soft and lightly browned.

2 Increase the heat and add the lamb. Cook for a further 5 minutes until the lamb is sealed. Add the curry powder, ground cinnamon and chilli flakes and cook for 2 minutes before adding the tomatoes and orange rind.

3 Stir the rice into the casserole then pour in the stock. Bring slowly to the boil and cover tightly. Transfer to the preheated oven and cook for 30–35 minutes until the rice is tender and the stock is absorbed.

4 Remove from the oven and leave to stand for 5 minutes before stirring in the chives and coriander. Season to taste with salt and pepper. Garnish with the lemon slices and sprigs of fresh coriander and serve immediately.

## Ingredients        SERVES 4

2 tbsp vegetable oil
25 g/1 oz flaked or slivered almonds
1 onion, peeled and finely chopped
1 carrot, peeled and finely chopped
1 celery stalk, trimmed and
    finely chopped
350 g/12 oz lean lamb, cut into chunks
2 tsp curry powder
$1/4$ tsp ground cinnamon
$1/4$ tsp dried chilli flakes
2 large tomatoes, skinned, deseeded
    and chopped
grated rind of 1 orange
350 g/12 oz easy-cook brown
    basmati rice
600 ml/1 pint vegetable or lamb stock
2 tbsp freshly snipped chives
3 tbsp freshly chopped coriander
salt and freshly ground black pepper

### To garnish:
lemon slices
sprigs of fresh coriander

# Lamb Biryani

1 Rinse the rice at least two or three times then reserve. Heat 1 tablespoon of the oil or ghee in a saucepan, add half the cloves and cardamom pods and fry for 30 seconds. Add half the rice and cover with boiling water. Bring to the boil, reduce the heat, cover and simmer for 12–15 minutes, or until the rice is tender. Drain and reserve. Cook the remaining rice, cloves, cardamom pods and the saffron strands in another saucepan. Drain and reserve.

2 Blend the yogurt, garlic, ginger, turmeric, ground coriander and cumin together with the lamb. Stir, cover and leave to marinate in the refrigerator for at least 2–3 hours.

3 When ready to cook, preheat the oven to 200°C/400°F/Gas Mark 6. Heat the remaining oil or ghee in a large saucepan, add the onions and fry for 5 minutes, or until softened. Add the tomatoes. Using a slotted spoon, remove the lamb from the marinade, reserving the marinade, and add the lamb to the pan. Cook, stirring, for 5 minutes then add the remaining marinade. Cover and cook, stirring occasionally, for 25–30 minutes, or until the lamb is tender and the sauce is thick. Stir in the herbs.

4 Oil an ovenproof dish. Spoon in a layer of plain rice and cover with a layer of saffron rice, then top with a layer of lamb. Repeat, finishing with a layer of rice. Cover with foil and place in the oven for 10 minutes. Invert onto a warmed plate and serve.

## Ingredients SERVES 4–6

250 g/9 oz basmati rice
4 tbsp vegetable oil or ghee
4 whole cloves
4 green cardamom pods, cracked
$1/4$ tsp saffron strands
120 ml/4 fl oz natural yogurt
2 garlic cloves, peeled and crushed
small piece fresh root ginger, peeled and grated
$1/2$ tsp turmeric
2–3 tsp ground coriander
2 tsp ground cumin
550 g/1$1/4$ lb boneless lean lamb, diced
2 onions, peeled and finely sliced
225 g/8 oz tomatoes, chopped
1 tbsp freshly chopped coriander
1 tbsp freshly chopped mint

## Food fact

Biryani is normally served as the main piece in a celebration meal and often would be made using goat or kid.

2

3

4

# Lamb Balti

1   Dice the lamb and reserve. Heat the oil or ghee in a large frying pan, add the mustard seeds and fry for 30 seconds, or until they pop.

2   Add the remaining spices and cook for 2 minutes, stirring, before adding the garlic, chillies, onions and aubergine. Cook, stirring, for a further 5 minutes, or until the vegetables are coated in the spices.

3   Add the lamb and continue to fry for 5–8 minutes, or until sealed. Stir in the chopped tomatoes. Blend the tomato purée with the stock then pour into the pan. Bring to the boil, cover, reduce the heat and simmer for 45–50 minutes, or until the lamb is tender. Sprinkle with chopped coriander and serve with plenty of naan bread.

## Ingredients    SERVES 4–6

450 g/1 lb lean lamb, such as
    fillet, trimmed
2 tbsp vegetable oil or ghee
1 tsp mustard seeds
1 tsp ground coriander
1 tsp ground cumin
$^{1}/_{2}$ tsp turmeric
$^{1}/_{2}$ tsp asafoetida
1 tsp garam masala
2–3 garlic cloves, peeled and crushed
2–3 green chillies, deseeded
    and chopped
2 onions, peeled and chopped
1 aubergine, trimmed and chopped
4 tomatoes, chopped
2 tsp tomato purée
600 ml/1 pint lamb or vegetable stock
2 tbsp freshly chopped coriander
naan bread, to serve

### Food fact
The Urdu pot that this is normally cooked in is known as a 'karahi'.

# Roghan Josh

1. Trim the lamb shanks of any excess fat, rinse, pat dry with absorbent kitchen paper and reserve. Heat the oil in a large pan, add the seeds, whole cloves and cinnamon stick and fry for 1 minute, stirring. Add the lamb shanks and cook on all sides until sealed. Remove and reserve. (If there is room the lamb could be left in the pan.)

2. Add the chillies, garlic and onions to the pan and continue to fry for 5–8 minutes, or until softened. Stir in the turmeric and curry leaves and cook for 2 minutes.

3. Add the tomatoes and stir well, then cook for 10 minutes, or until the tomatoes have collapsed. Return the lamb shanks to the pan, if reserved, and add enough water to half cover the lamb. Bring to the boil, then reduce the heat, cover and simmer for 1¹/₂–2 hours, or until tender. Remove the shanks from the pan and keep warm.

4. Discard the cinnamon stick then blend the sauce in a food processor until smooth. Reheat for 2 minutes then pour over the lamb and sprinkle with chopped coriander. Serve.

## Ingredients          SERVES 4–6

4 lamb shanks
2 tbsp vegetable oil
1 tsp fennel seeds
1 tsp mustard seeds
2 whole cloves
1 cinnamon stick, bruised
2 red chillies, deseeded and chopped
4 garlic cloves, peeled and crushed
225 g/8 oz onions, peeled and chopped
1 tsp turmeric
few curry leaves
4 tomatoes, chopped
2 tbsp freshly chopped coriander

### Tasty tip

If liked, this dish can be made with skinless, boneless lamb. Also, try stirring in 2 tablespoons ground almonds into the sauce in step 4.

# Madras Lamb

1 Trim the lamb and cut into small chunks. Heat the oil in a saucepan, add the mustard seeds and crushed chillies and fry for 1–2 minutes.

2 Add the remaining spices with the garlic and ginger and cook, stirring, for 5 minutes.

3 Add the meat and onion to the pan and cook, stirring, until coated in the spices.

4 Blend the tomato purée with the stock and pour into the pan. Bring to the boil, then reduce the heat, cover and simmer for 40 minutes, or until the meat is tender. Sprinkle with the chopped coriander and serve with freshly cooked basmati rice.

## Ingredients    SERVES 4–6

450 g/1 lb lean lamb, such as fillet
2 tbsp vegetable oil
1 tsp black mustard seeds
1 tbsp dried crushed chillies
1 tsp ground cumin
1 tsp ground coriander
1 tsp paprika
1 tsp turmeric
2–4 garlic cloves, peeled and crushed
5 cm/2 inch fresh root ginger, peeled and grated
1 onion, peeled and chopped
1 tbsp tomato purée
450 ml/³/₄ pint lamb stock
1 tbsp freshly chopped coriander
freshly cooked basmati rice, to serve

### Helpful hint

Dried chillies have a more intensive flavour and a higher heat content. As the dish cooks, the heat and flavour increase so take care how much you use.

# Slow-roasted Lamb

1 Preheat the oven to 190°C/375°F/Gas Mark 5. Wipe the lamb with absorbent kitchen paper and make small slits over the lamb. Reserve.

2 Heat the oil in a frying pan, add the seeds and fry for 30 seconds, stirring. Add the remaining spices including the 2 garlic cloves and green chillies and cook for 5 minutes. Remove and use half to spread over the lamb.

3 Cut the potatoes into bite-sized chunks and the onions into wedges. Cut the garlic in half. Place in a roasting tin and cover with the remaining spice paste, then place the lamb on top.

4 Cook in the preheated oven for 1¼–1½ hours, or until the lamb and potatoes are cooked. Turn the potatoes over occasionally during cooking. Serve the lamb with the potatoes and freshly cooked vegetables.

## Ingredients        SERVES 6

1 leg of lamb, about 1.5 kg/3 lb
   in weight
2 tbsp vegetable oil
1 tsp fennel seeds
1 tsp cumin seeds
1 tsp ground coriander
1 tsp turmeric
2 garlic cloves, peeled and crushed
2 green chillies, deseeded
   and chopped
freshly cooked vegetables, to serve

### For the potatoes:

550 g/1¼ lb potatoes, peeled
2 onions, peeled
4 garlic cloves, peeled

### Tasty tip

Roasted assorted peppers, aubergine and courgettes would be perfect to serve with this dish. Trim and dice the vegetables, pour over 2 tablespoons of oil and roast with the lamb for the last 35 minutes of cooking time.

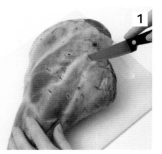

# Lamb & Potato Curry

1. Discard any fat or gristle from the lamb, then cut into thin strips and reserve.

2. Heat the oil in a deep frying pan, add the onions, garlic and celery and fry for 5 minutes, or until softened. Add the ginger, chillies, curry leaves and spices and continue to fry for a further 3 minutes, stirring constantly. Add the lamb and cook for 5 minutes, or until coated in the spices.

3. Blend the tomato purée with the water then stir into the pan together with the coconut milk and chopped tomatoes.

4. Cut the potatoes into small chunks and add to the pan with the carrots. Bring to the boil, then reduce the heat, cover and simmer for 25–30 minutes, or until the lamb and vegetables are tender.

## Ingredients        SERVES 4

450 g/1 lb lean lamb, such as
   leg steaks
2 tbsp vegetable oil
2 onions, peeled and cut into wedges
2–3 garlic cloves, peeled and sliced
2 celery sticks, trimmed and sliced
5 cm/2 inch piece fresh root ginger,
   peeled and grated
2 green chillies, deseeded
   and chopped
few curry leaves
1 tsp ground cumin
1 tsp ground coriander
1 tsp turmeric
1 tbsp tomato purée
150 ml/$^{1}/_{4}$ pint water
150 ml/$^{1}/_{4}$ pint coconut milk
225 g/8 oz tomatoes, chopped
450 g/1 lb new potatoes, scrubbed
100 g/4 oz carrots, peeled and sliced

# Kashmir Lamb

1 Discard any fat or gristle from the meat, cut into small chunks and reserve. Heat the oil or ghee in a large heavy-based frying pan, add the onions, garlic, ginger and cinnamon stick and cook for 5 minutes, or until the onions have softened. Add the remaining spices and cook for a further 3 minutes, stirring.

2 Add the meat to the pan and cook, stirring, until lightly coated in the spices.

3 Stir in the stock. Bring to the boil, then reduce the heat, cover and simmer for 20 minutes, stirring occasionally.

4 Stir the yogurt and ground almonds into the pan and continue to simmer for 15 minutes, or until the meat is tender. Stir in the cream, bring to just below boiling point and heat for 3 minutes. Spoon into a warmed serving dish, sprinkle with the chopped nuts and serve.

## Ingredients          SERVES 4–6

550 g/1¼ lb lean lamb,
    such as leg steaks
2 tbsp vegetable oil or ghee
2 red onions, peeled and chopped
3–4 garlic cloves, peeled and crushed
small piece fresh root ginger, peeled
    and grated
1 cinnamon stick, bruised
1½ tsp ground cumin
1½ tsp ground coriander
1 tsp turmeric
1 tsp chilli powder
450 ml/¾ pint lamb or vegetable stock
150 ml/¼ pint natural yogurt
2 tbsp ground almonds
2–3 tbsp single cream
25 g/1 oz unsalted cashew nuts,
    roughly chopped
25 g/1 oz pistachio nuts, shelled if
    necessary, and chopped

### Helpful hint
Adding the almonds with the yogurt
helps to prevent the sauce curdling.

# Lamb Passanda

1 Discard any fat or gristle from the lamb, cut into thin strips and reserve. Heat the oil or ghee in a large frying pan, add the spices including the cinnamon and cloves and cook for 3 minutes.

2 Add the ginger, chillies, garlic, onions and meat and cook, stirring, until the meat is coated in the spices.

3 Stir in the yogurt then spoon into a bowl, cover and leave to marinate in the refrigerator for 15 minutes.

4 Clean the pan and return the meat mixture to it together with the water. Bring to the boil, then reduce the heat, cover and simmer for 15 minutes.

5 Pour in the coconut cream and add the green pepper and sultanas. Stir in the ground almonds. Return to the boil, then reduce the heat and simmer for 20 minutes, or until the meat is tender. Spoon into a warmed serving dish, sprinkle with the nuts and serve.

## Ingredients     SERVES 4–6

550 g/1¼ lb lean lamb, such as leg steaks
2 tbsp vegetable oil or ghee
1 tsp ground cumin
1 tsp ground coriander
1 tsp turmeric
½ tsp fenugreek seeds
3 green cardamom pods, cracked
1 cinnamon stick, bruised
3 whole cloves
5 cm/2 inch piece fresh root ginger, peeled and grated
1–2 green chillies, deseeded and finely chopped
2–4 garlic cloves, peeled and crushed
2 red onions, peeled and chopped
150 ml/¼ pint natural yogurt
250 ml/8 fl oz water
85 ml/3 fl oz coconut cream
1 green pepper, deseeded and cut into strips
50 g/2 oz sultanas
3 tbsp ground almonds
25 g/1 oz blanched almonds
25 g/1 oz unsalted cashews, chopped

# Spicy Pork

1 Heat a wok or large frying pan, add 2 tablespoons of the oil and, when hot, add the ginger, garlic, carrots and aubergine and stir-fry for 2 minutes. Using a slotted spoon, transfer to a plate and keep warm.

2 Add the remaining oil to the wok, heat until smoking, then add the pork and stir-fry for 5–8 minutes or until browned all over. Transfer to a plate and keep warm. Wipe the wok clean.

3 Pour half the coconut milk into the wok, stir in the red curry paste and bring to the boil. Boil rapidly for 4 minutes, stirring occasionally, or until the sauce is reduced by half.

4 Add the fish sauce and sugar to the wok and bring back to the boil. Return the pork and vegetables to the wok with the bamboo shoots. Return to the boil, then simmer for 4 minutes.

5 Stir in the remaining coconut milk and season to taste with salt. Simmer for 2 minutes or until heated through. Garnish with lime zest and serve immediately with rice.

## Ingredients    SERVES 4

4 tbsp groundnut oil
2.5 cm/1 inch piece fresh root ginger, peeled and cut into matchsticks
1 garlic clove, peeled and chopped
2 carrots, peeled and cut into matchsticks
1 aubergine, trimmed and cubed
550 g/1¼ lb pork fillet, thickly sliced
400 ml/14 oz can coconut milk
2 tbsp Thai red curry paste
1-2 tbsp, or to taste, Thai fish sauce
2 tsp caster sugar
227 g/8 oz can bamboo shoots in brine, drained and cut into matchsticks
salt, to taste
lime zest, to garnish
freshly cooked rice, to serve

# Pork with Tofu & Coconut

1 Place the cashew nuts, coriander, cumin, chilli powder, ginger and oyster sauce in a food processor and blend until finely ground. Heat a wok or large frying pan, add 2 tablespoons of the oil and, when hot, add the cashew mixture and stir-fry for 1 minute. Stir in the coconut milk, bring to the boil, then simmer for 1 minute. Pour into a small jug and reserve. Wipe the wok clean.

2 Meanwhile, place the rice noodles in a bowl, cover with boiling water, leave to stand for 5 minutes, then drain thoroughly.

3 Reheat the wok, add the remaining oil and, when hot, add the pork and stir-fry for 5 minutes or until browned all over. Add the chillies and spring onions and stir-fry for 2 minutes.

4 Add the tomatoes and tofu to the wok with the noodles and coconut mixture and stir-fry for a further 2 minutes, or until heated through, being careful not to break up the tofu. Sprinkle with the chopped coriander and mint, season to taste with salt and pepper and stir. Tip into a warmed serving dish and serve immediately.

## Ingredients          SERVES 4

50 g/2 oz unsalted cashew nuts
1 tbsp ground coriander
1 tbsp ground cumin
2 tsp hot chilli powder
2.5 cm/1 inch piece fresh root
    ginger, peeled and chopped
1 tbsp oyster sauce
4 tbsp groundnut oil
400 ml/14 oz can coconut milk
175 g/6 oz rice noodles
450 g/1 lb pork tenderloin,
    thickly sliced
1 red chilli, deseeded and sliced
1 green chilli, deseeded and sliced
1 bunch spring onions, trimmed and
    thickly sliced
3 tomatoes, roughly chopped
75 g/3 oz tofu, drained and diced
2 tbsp freshly chopped coriander
2 tbsp freshly chopped mint
salt and freshly ground black pepper

# Kerala Pork Curry

1 Cut the pork into small chunks and reserve. Heat 1 teaspoon of the oil or ghee in a frying pan, add the coconut and fry for 30 seconds, stirring, until lightly toasted. Reserve.

2 Add the remaining oil or ghee to the pan, add the seeds and fry for 30 seconds, or until they pop. Add the remaining spices and cook, stirring, for 2 minutes. Add the pork and fry for 5 minutes, or until sealed

3 Add the chillies, garlic and onions and continue to fry for 3 minutes before stirring in the saffron strands. Stir then pour in the coconut milk and water.

4 Bring to the boil then reduce the heat, cover and simmer, stirring occasionally, for 30 minutes. Add a little more water if the liquid is evaporating quickly. Turn the heat down slightly, then add the peas and cook for a further 10 minutes before serving with freshly cooked basmati rice.

## Ingredients      SERVES 4–6

450 g/1 lb pork loin, trimmed
2 tbsp vegetable oil or ghee
1 tbsp desiccated coconut
1 tsp mustard seeds
1 tsp fennel seeds
1 cinnamon stick, bruised
1 tsp ground cumin
1 tsp ground coriander
1–2 red chillies, deseeded
   and chopped
2–3 garlic cloves, peeled
   and chopped
2 onions, peeled and chopped
$^1/_2$ tsp saffron strands
300 ml/$^1/_2$ pint coconut milk
150 ml/$^1/_4$ pint water
100 g/4 oz frozen peas
freshly cooked basmati rice, to serve

## Helpful hint

Remember when handling chillies to handle with care and to wash your hands thoroughly before touching any sensitive parts.

# Vietnamese-style Braised Pork

1 Trim the pork and cut into 4 portions. Heat the oil in a large saucepan or frying pan, add the pork and brown on all sides. Remove and reserve.

2 Place the reserved pork, spring onions, ginger, lemon grass, chillies and lime leaves in a clean saucepan and add the stock and honey. Bring to the boil, then reduce the heat and simmer for 30 minutes, or until tender.

3 Add salt and pepper to taste with the fish sauce, then serve the pork sprinkled with chopped coriander on a bed of rice with the stir-fried vegetables.

## Ingredients          SERVES 4–6

550 g/1¼ lb pork tenderloin
2 tbsp vegetable oil
6 spring onions, trimmed and halved
5 cm/2 inch piece fresh root
    ginger, chopped
2 lemon grass stalks, bruised, outer
    leaves discarded
2–4 bird's eye chillies, deseeded
2 kaffir lime leaves
600 ml/1 pint chicken or
    vegetable stock
1 tbsp clear honey
salt and freshly ground black pepper
1 tbsp fish sauce, or to taste
1 tbsp freshly chopped coriander

**To serve:**
freshly cooked fragrant rice
stir-fried vegetables

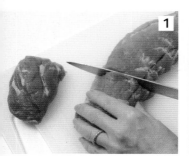

# Pork Creole

**1** Preheat the oven to 190°C/375°F/Gas Mark 5. Place all the ingredients for the sauce in a food processor and blend until smooth.

**2** Trim the fillet and, if liked, cut in half. Place the meat in a shallow roasting tin and brush with the prepared sauce. Cover lightly and store in the refrigerator until required. When ready to cook, remove the meat from the refrigerator, allow to return to room temperature, then place in the preheated oven and roast for 30 minutes, or until thoroughly cooked. Slice and keep warm.

**3** Meanwhile, heat the oil in a large frying pan, add the garlic, chillies, curry paste and leeks and cook, stirring, for 5 minutes before adding the rice. Continue to cook, stirring, for a further 5 minutes.

**4** Add half the stock, bring to the boil, then reduce the heat, cover and simmer for 10 minutes, stirring frequently. Add the chopped beans together with a little more stock and cook for a further 10 minutes, or until the rice is tender. Add more stock as necessary. Stir in the carrot, black pepper to taste and spring onions. Sprinkle with chopped coriander and serve with the sliced pork fillet.

## Ingredients
SERVES 4–6

**For the jerk sauce:**

2 tsp ground allspice; 50 g/2 oz light muscovado sugar; 6 garlic cloves, peeled; 2–4 Scotch bonnet chillies, deseeded; 2 tbsp freshly chopped thyme; 8 spring onions, trimmed and chopped; 1 tsp ground cinnamon; $\frac{1}{4}$ tsp freshly grated nutmeg; salt and freshly ground black pepper; 2 tbsp soy sauce; 1 whole pork fillet, about 700 g/1$\frac{1}{2}$ lb in weight

**For the spicy rice:**

1 tbsp olive oil; 2–3 garlic cloves, peeled and sliced; 1–2 red chillies, deseeded and chopped; 1–2 tbsp curry paste; 2 leeks, about 200 g/ 7 oz in weight, trimmed, sliced and thoroughly washed; 300 g/10 oz basmati rice; 750 ml/1$\frac{1}{4}$ pints vegetable stock; 225 g/8 oz French beans, trimmed and chopped; 1 large carrot, peeled and grated; 4 spring onions, trimmed and chopped; 2 tbsp freshly chopped coriander (optional)

# Pepper-Pot Stew

1 Trim the pork and beef discarding any fat or gristle, cut into thin strips and reserve. Heat the oil in a large saucepan, add the onion, celery and garlic and sauté for 5 minutes, or until beginning to soften. Add the chillies and spices and continue to cook for 3 minutes before adding the meat strips.

2 Cook, stirring, until the meat is coated in the spices, then stir in the chopped tomatoes. Blend the tomato purée with a little stock and stir into the pan with the remaining stock. Bring to the boil, then reduce the heat, cover and simmer, stirring occasionally, for 1½–2 hours, or until the meat is tender. If the liquid is evaporating too quickly, reduce the heat and add a little more stock.

3 Adjust the seasoning adding some hot pepper sauce, if liked, and sprinkle with chopped coriander. Serve with a sweet chutney and freshly cooked rice and peas.

## Ingredients          SERVES 4–6

450 g/1 lb lean pork, such as fillet
225 g/8 oz lean braising steak
2 tbsp vegetable oil
1 onion, peeled and chopped
2 celery sticks, trimmed and sliced
4 garlic cloves, peeled and chopped
1–2 habanero chillies, deseeded
    and chopped
1 tsp ground allspice
½ tsp ground cloves
1 tsp ground cinnamon
450 g/1 lb ripe tomatoes, chopped
1 tbsp tomato purée
300 ml/½ pint beef stock
salt and freshly ground black pepper
hot pepper sauce, to taste (optional)
1 tbsp freshly chopped coriander

### To serve:
sweet chutney
freshly cooked rice
freshly cooked peas

# Pork Vindaloo

1   Soak the dried chillies in plenty of hot water and leave for 1 hour, or longer if time permits. Place the onion in a small saucepan and cover with water. Bring to the boil, then reduce the heat, cover and simmer for 15 minutes, or until very soft. Take care not to allow all the water to evaporate otherwise the onion will burn. Using a slotted spoon, remove the dried chillies and chop. Reserve.

2   Grind the cloves, cinnamon stick and cumin seeds until fine. Place the ginger, garlic, pepper, tamarind paste, sugar, vinegar, all the chillies and the onion in a food processor and blend to a smooth paste.

3   Cut the pork into small chunks and reserve. Heat the oil in a heavy-based saucepan, add the pork and brown on all sides. Add the prepared curry paste and stir until the pork is well coated in the paste. Pour in the stock and tomatoes. Bring to the boil, then reduce the heat, cover and simmer, stirring occasionally, for 1½–2 hours, or until tender. Add a little extra stock if necessary. Sprinkle with chopped coriander and serve with freshly cooked rice.

## Ingredients     SERVES 4–6

2 dried red chillies
1 small onion, peeled and chopped
5 whole cloves
1 small cinnamon stick, bruised
1 tsp cumin seeds
small piece fresh root ginger, peeled and grated
4 garlic cloves, peeled and chopped
1 tsp freshly ground black pepper
1 tsp tamarind paste
1 tsp sugar
2 tbsp white wine vinegar
2–4 hot red chillies, deseeded
550 g/1¼ lb pork fillet trimmed
2 tbsp vegetable oil
300 ml/½ pint beef stock
225 g/8 oz ripe tomatoes, chopped
2 tbsp freshly chopped coriander
freshly cooked rice, to serve

## Helpful hint

This is a seriously hot curry. Dried chillies are always far hotter than fresh. Remember that the hottest part is in the seed membrane as well as the seeds.

# Poultry

If your game is poultry than these are the curries for you! From restaurant favourites like Chicken Tikka Masala and Tandoori Chicken to the exotic Calypso Chicken & Coconut Stew – there is something for everyone among this scrumptious selection. Not into chicken? Green Turkey Curry or Duck Curry is a succulent substitute.

# Chicken Tikka Masala

**1** Preheat the oven to 200°C/400°F/Gas Mark 6, 15 minutes before cooking. Cut each chicken breast across into 3 pieces, then make 2 or 3 shallow cuts in each piece. Put in a shallow dish. Mix together the yogurt, garlic, ginger, chilli powder, ground coriander and lime juice. Pour over the chicken, cover and marinate in the refrigerator for up to 24 hours.

**2** Remove the chicken from the marinade and arrange on an oiled baking tray. Bake in the preheated oven for 15 minutes, or until golden brown and cooked.

**3** While the chicken is cooking, heat the butter or ghee and oil in a wok and stir-fry the onion for 5 minutes, or until tender. Add the chilli and garam masala and stir-fry for a few more seconds. Stir in the cream and remaining marinade. Simmer over a low heat for 1 minute, stirring all the time.

**4** Add the chicken pieces and cook for a further 1 minute, stirring to coat in the sauce. Season to taste with salt and pepper. Transfer the chicken pieces to a warmed serving plate. Stir the chopped coriander into the sauce, then spoon over the chicken, garnish and serve immediately with freshly cooked rice.

## Ingredients
SERVES 4

4 skinless chicken breast fillets
150 ml/$^1/_4$ pint natural yogurt
1 garlic clove, peeled and crushed
2.5 cm/1 inch piece fresh root ginger, peeled and grated
1 tsp chilli powder
1 tbsp ground coriander
2 tbsp lime juice
twist of lime, to garnish
freshly cooked rice, to serve

## For the masala sauce:

15 g/$^1/_2$ oz unsalted butter or ghee
2 tbsp vegetable oil
1 onion, peeled and chopped
1 green chilli, deseeded and finely chopped
1 tsp garam masala
150 ml/$^1/_4$ pint double cream
salt and freshly ground black pepper
3 tbsp fresh coriander leaves, roughly torn

# Thai Red Chicken Curry

1 Pour the coconut cream into a small saucepan and heat gently. Meanwhile, heat a wok or large frying pan and add the oil. When the oil is very hot, swirl the oil around the wok until the wok is lightly coated, then add the garlic and stir-fry for about 10–20 seconds, or until the garlic begins to brown. Add the curry paste and stir-fry for a few more seconds, then pour in the warmed coconut cream.

2 Cook the coconut cream mixture for 5 minutes, or until the cream has curdled and thickened. Stir in the fish sauce and sugar. Add the finely sliced chicken breast and cook for 3–4 minutes, or until the chicken has turned white.

3 Pour the stock into the wok, bring to the boil, then simmer for 1–2 minutes, or until the chicken is cooked through. Stir in the shredded lime leaves. Turn into a warmed serving dish, garnish with chopped red chilli and serve immediately with rice.

## Ingredients        SERVES 4

250 ml/8 fl oz coconut cream
2 tbsp vegetable oil
2 garlic cloves, peeled and
   finely chopped
2 tbsp Thai red curry paste
2 tbsp Thai fish sauce
2 tsp sugar
350 g/12 oz boneless, skinless
   chicken breast, finely sliced
450 ml/3/4 pint chicken stock
2 kaffir lime leaves, shredded
chopped red chilli, to garnish
steamed Thai fragrant rice, to serve

# Thai Green Chicken Curry

1 Place the onion, lemon grass, garlic, ginger, chillies, lime rind and juice, 1 tablespoon of groundnut oil, the fish sauce, coriander and basil in a food processor. Blend to form a smooth paste, which should be of a dropping consistency. If the sauce looks thick, add a little water. Remove and reserve.

2 Heat the wok, add the remaining 1 tablespoon of oil and, when hot, add the chicken. Stir-fry for 2–3 minutes, until the chicken starts to colour, then add the green beans and stir-fry for a further minute. Remove the chicken and beans from the wok and reserve. Wipe the wok clean with absorbent kitchen paper.

3 Spoon the reserved green paste into the wok and heat for 1 minute. Add the coconut milk and whisk to blend. Return the chicken and beans to the wok and bring to the boil. Simmer for 5–7 minutes, or until the chicken is cooked. Sprinkle with basil leaves and serve immediately with freshly cooked rice.

## Ingredients SERVES 4

1 onion, peeled and chopped
3 lemon grass stalks, finely sliced and
    outer leaves discarded
2 garlic cloves, peeled and
    finely chopped
1 tbsp freshly grated root ginger
3 green chillies
rind and juice of 1 lime
2 tbsp groundnut oil
2 tbsp Thai fish sauce
6 tbsp freshly chopped coriander
6 tbsp freshly chopped Thai basil
450 g/1 lb skinless, boneless chicken
    breasts, cut into strips
125 g /4 oz fine green beans, trimmed
400 ml/14 oz can coconut milk
fresh Thai basil leaves, to garnish
freshly cooked Thai fragrant rice,
    to serve

### Tasty tip

Use Thai holy basil in this recipe if possible. The leaves are flatter and coarser than Italian basil with a stronger, more pronounced aniseed flavour.

# Chicken & Red Pepper Curried Rice

1 Wash the rice in several changes of water until the water remains relatively clear. Drain well. Put into a saucepan and cover with fresh water. Add a little salt and bring to the boil. Cook for 12-15 minutes until tender. Drain and refresh under cold running water, then drain again and reserve.

2 Lightly whisk the egg white with 1 teaspoon of salt and 2 teaspoons of cornflour until smooth. Add the chicken and mix together well. Cover and chill in the refrigerator for 20 minutes.

3 Heat the wok then add the oil and heat until moderately hot. Add the chicken mixture to the wok and stir-fry for 2–3 minutes until all the chicken has turned white. Using a slotted spoon, lift the cubes of chicken from the wok, then drain on absorbent kitchen paper.

4 Add the red pepper to the wok and stir-fry for 1 minute over a high heat. Add the curry powder or paste and cook for a further 30 seconds, then add the chicken stock, sugar, Chinese rice wine or dry sherry and soy sauce.

5 Mix the remaining cornflour with 1 teaspoon cold water and add to the wok, stirring. Bring to the boil and simmer gently for 1 minute. Return the chicken to the wok, simmer for a further minute, then add the rice. Stir over a medium heat until heated through. Garnish with the coriander and serve.

## Ingredients          SERVES 4

350 g/12 oz long-grain rice
salt
1 large egg white
1 tbsp cornflour
300 g/10 oz skinless chicken breast
    fillets, cut into chunks
3 tbsp groundnut oil
1 red pepper, deseeded and
    roughly chopped
1 tbsp curry powder or paste
125 ml/4 fl oz chicken stock
1 tsp sugar
1 tbsp Chinese rice wine or
    dry sherry
1 tbsp light soy sauce
sprigs of fresh coriander, to garnish

## Helpful hint

When stir-frying it is important to maintain a steady high heat and to keep the food on the move. This ensures that all the food is cooked and does not stick to the wok. Use a large flat cooking spoon or a bamboo paddle for this.

# Aromatic Chicken Curry

1 Put the lentils in a sieve and rinse thoroughly under cold running water.

2 Dry-fry the ground coriander and cumin seeds in a large saucepan over a low heat for about 30 seconds. Stir in the curry paste.

3 Add the lentils to the saucepan with the bay leaf and lemon rind, then pour in the stock.

4 Stir, then slowly bring to the boil. Turn down the heat, half-cover the pan with a lid and simmer gently for 5 minutes, stirring occasionally.

5 Secure the chicken thighs with cocktail sticks to keep their shape. Place in the pan and half-cover. Simmer for 15 minutes.

6 Stir in the shredded spinach and cook for a further 25 minutes or until the chicken is very tender and the sauce is thick.

7 Remove the bay leaf and lemon rind. Stir in the coriander and lemon juice, then season to taste with salt and pepper. Serve immediately with the rice and a little natural yogurt.

## Ingredients                     SERVES 4

125 g/4 oz red lentils
2 tsp ground coriander
$1/_2$ tsp cumin seeds
2 tsp mild curry paste
1 bay leaf
small strip lemon rind
600 ml/1 pint chicken or
    vegetable stock
8 chicken thighs, skinned
175 g/6 oz spinach leaves, rinsed
    and shredded
1 tbsp freshly chopped coriander
2 tsp lemon juice
salt and freshly ground black pepper

**To serve:**
freshly cooked rice
low-fat natural yogurt

**Helpful hint**
Dry-frying spices really releases the flavour of the spices and is a technique that can be used in many dishes.

# Thai Coconut Chicken

1 Heat the wok and add the cumin seeds, mustard seeds and coriander seeds. Dry-fry over a low to medium heat for 2 minutes, or until the fragrance becomes stronger and the seeds start to pop. Add the turmeric and leave to cool slightly. Grind the spices in a pestle and mortar or blend to a fine powder in a food processor.

2 Mix the chilli, ginger, garlic and the cream together in a small bowl, add the ground spices and mix. Place the chicken thighs in a shallow dish and spread the spice paste over the thighs.

3 Heat the wok over a high heat, add the oil and, when hot, add the onion and stir-fry until golden brown. Add the chicken and spice paste. Cook for 5–6 minutes, stirring occasionally, until evenly coloured. Add the coconut milk and season to taste with salt and pepper. Simmer the chicken for 15–20 minutes, or until the thighs are cooked through, taking care not to allow the mixture to boil. Stir in the chopped coriander and serve immediately with the freshly cooked rice sprinkled with shredded spring onions.

## Ingredients          SERVES 4

1 tsp cumin seeds
1 tsp mustard seeds
1 tsp coriander seeds
1 tsp turmeric
1 bird's eye chilli, deseeded and
    finely chopped
1 tbsp freshly grated root ginger
2 garlic cloves, peeled and
    finely chopped
125 ml/4 fl oz double cream
8 skinless chicken thighs
2 tbsp groundnut oil
1 onion, peeled and finely sliced
200 ml/7 fl oz coconut milk
salt and freshly ground black pepper
4 tbsp freshly chopped coriander
2 spring onions, shredded, to garnish
freshly cooked Thai fragrant rice,
    to serve

# Spicy Persian Chicken

**1** Heat the oil in a large heavy-based saucepan over a medium-high heat. Cook the chicken pieces, in batches, until lightly browned. Return all the chicken to the saucepan.

**2** Add the onions to the saucepan, reduce the heat to medium and cook for 3–5 minutes, stirring frequently, until the onions begin to soften. Add the garlic, ginger, turmeric, chilli powder, coriander, cumin and rice and stir to coat the rice.

**3** Cook for about 2 minutes until the rice is golden and translucent. Stir in the tomato purée and the saffron strands, then season to taste with salt and pepper.

**4** Add the pomegranate juice and stock and bring to the boil, stirring once or twice. Add the apricots or prunes and raisins and stir gently. Reduce the heat to low and cook for 30 minutes until the chicken and rice are tender and the liquid is absorbed.

**5** Turn into a shallow serving dish and sprinkle with the chopped coriander. Serve immediately, garnished with pomegranate seeds, if using.

## Ingredients SERVES 4

2–3 tbsp vegetable oil

700 g/1½ lb boneless skinless chicken pieces (breast and thighs), cut into 2.5 cm/1 inch pieces

2 onions, peeled and coarsely chopped

2 garlic cloves, peeled and finely chopped

2.5 cm/1 inch piece root ginger, chopped

1 tsp ground turmeric

½ tsp chilli powder

1 tsp ground coriander

1 tsp ground cumin

200 g/7 oz long-grain white rice

1 tbsp tomato purée

1 tsp saffron strands

salt and freshly ground black pepper

100 ml/3½ fl oz pomegranate juice

900 ml/1½ pints chicken stock

125 g/4 oz ready-to-eat dried apricots or prunes, halved

2 tbsp raisins

2 tbsp freshly chopped coriander

pomegranate seeds, to garnish (optional)

# Creamy Chicken & Rice

**1** Bring a saucepan of lightly salted water to the boil. Gradually pour in the rice; return to the boil, then simmer for about 12 minutes until tender. Drain, rinse under cold water and reserve.

**2** Heat the ghee or butter in a large deep frying pan over a medium-high heat. Add the almonds and pistachios and cook for about 2 minutes, stirring constantly, until golden. Using a slotted spoon, transfer to a plate.

**3** Add the chicken pieces to the pan and cook for 5 minutes, or until golden, turning once. Remove from the pan and reserve. Add the oil to the pan and cook the onions for 10 minutes, or until golden, stirring frequently. Stir in the garlic, ginger and spices and cook for 2–3 minutes, stirring.

**4** Add 2–3 tablespoons of the yogurt and cook, stirring until the moisture evaporates. Continue adding the yogurt in this way until it is used up.

**5** Return the chicken and nuts to the pan and stir. Stir in 125 ml/4 fl oz of boiling water and season to taste with salt and pepper. Cook, covered, over a low heat for 10 minutes until the chicken is tender. Stir in the cream, grapes and half the herbs. Gently fold in the rice. Heat through for 5 minutes and sprinkle with the remaining herbs, then serve.

## Ingredients     SERVES 4

350 g/12 oz basmati rice
50 g/2 oz ghee or unsalted butter
100 g/3$^1/_2$ oz flaked almonds
75 g/3 oz unsalted shelled
 pistachio nuts
4–6 skinless chicken breast fillets,
 each cut into 4 pieces
2 tbsp groundnut oil
2 onions, peeled and thinly sliced
2 garlic cloves, peeled and chopped
2.5 cm/1 inch piece fresh root
 ginger, finely chopped
6 green cardamom pods, lightly cracked
4–6 whole cloves
1 tsp ground cumin
$^1/_2$ tsp cayenne pepper, or to taste
225 ml/8 fl oz natural yogurt
salt and freshly ground black pepper
225 ml/8 fl oz double cream
225 g/8 oz seedless green grapes,
 halved if large
2 bay leaves
1 tsp ground coriander
2 tbsp freshly chopped
 coriander or mint

# Spicy Chicken Skewers with Mango Tabbouleh

**1** If using wooden skewers, pre-soak them in cold water for at least 30 minutes. (This stops them from burning during grilling.)

**2** Cut the chicken into 5 x 1 cm/2 x ¹/₂ inch strips and place in a shallow dish. Mix together the yogurt, garlic, chilli, turmeric, curry powder, lemon rind and juice. Pour over the chicken and toss to coat. Cover and leave to marinate in the refrigerator for up to 8 hours.

**3** To make the tabbouleh, put the bulgur wheat in a bowl. Pour over enough boiling water to cover. Put a plate over the bowl. Leave to soak for 20 minutes.

**4** Whisk together the oil and lemon juice in a bowl. Add the red onion and leave to marinate for 10 minutes. Drain the bulgur wheat and squeeze out any excess moisture in a clean tea towel. Add to the red onion with the mango, cucumber and herbs and season to taste with salt and pepper. Toss together.

**5** Thread the chicken strips onto 8 wooden or metal skewers. Cook under a hot grill for 12-15 minutes or until thoroughly cooked. Turn the skewers over and brush with the remaining marinade during cooking. Spoon the tabbouleh onto individual plates. Arrange the chicken skewers on top and garnish with the sprigs of mint. Serve warm or cold.

## Ingredients          SERVES 4

400 g/14 oz chicken breast fillet
200 ml/7 fl oz natural low fat yogurt
1 garlic clove, peeled and crushed
1 small red chilli, deseeded and
    finely chopped
¹/₂ tsp ground turmeric
1-2 tsp or to taste curry powder
finely grated rind and juice
    ¹/₂ lemon
sprigs of fresh mint, to garnish

### For the mango tabbouleh:

175 g/6 oz bulgur wheat
1 tsp olive oil
juice ¹/₂ lemon
¹/₂ red onion, peeled and
    finely chopped
1 ripe mango, halved, stoned, peeled
    and chopped
¹/₄ cucumber, finely diced
2 tbsp freshly chopped parsley
2 tbsp freshly shredded mint
salt and finely ground black pepper

# Caribbean Style Chicken Stew

1 Lightly rinse the chicken and dry with absorbent kitchen paper. Heat the oil in a large saucepan, add the chicken and brown on all sides. Remove and reserve.

2 Chop the celery and add to the pan with the onions, garlic and chillies. Sauté for 5–8 minutes, or until lightly browned. Add all the spices and cook for a further 3 minutes. Add the sugar, tomatoes and stock and bring to the boil.

3 Return the chicken to the pan, then reduce the heat, cover and simmer for 1 hour, or until the chicken is tender. Spoon into a warmed serving dish, sprinkle with chopped coriander and serve with the sweet potato mash.

## Ingredients    SERVES 4–6

4 skinless, boneless chicken portions, each about 100 g/4 oz in weight
2 tbsp groundnut oil
2 celery sticks, trimmed
6 baby onions, peeled and halved
2–4 garlic cloves, peeled and sliced
1–2 Habanero chillies, deseeded and sliced
1 tsp ground cumin
1 tsp ground coriander
1 tsp ground allspice
1 tsp turmeric
2 tsp demerara sugar
225 g/8 oz tomatoes, chopped
600 ml/1 pint chicken stock
1 tbsp freshly chopped coriander
sweet potato mash, to serve

### Tasty tip

This dish is quite fiery, but the impact can be increased by adding a few dashes of Hot Pepper Sauce at the end of cooking.

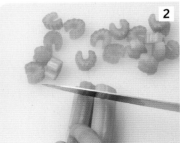

# Calypso Chicken

1 Peel the onions and, keeping the root intact, cut into thin wedges. Heat the oil in a heavy-based saucepan, add the chicken and brown on all sides. Remove from the pan and reserve.

2 Add the onions, garlic and chillies to the pan and sauté for 5–8 minutes, or until lightly browned. Sprinkle in all the spices and cook, stirring, for 2 minutes.

3 Return the chicken to the pan and stir in the coconut milk and stock. Bring to the boil, then reduce the heat, cover and simmer for 30 minutes.

4 Add the peppers and continue to simmer for 15 minutes, or until the chicken is cooked. Spoon into a warmed serving dish, sprinkle with toasted coconut or chopped coriander and serve with rice.

## Ingredients          SERVES 4–6

2 onions
2 tbsp groundnut oil
450 g/1 lb skinless, boneless chicken breast, diced
2–4 garlic cloves, peeled and sliced
1–2 chillies, deseeded and sliced
1 tsp ground coriander
1 tsp ground cumin
1 tsp turmeric
1 tsp ground allspice
400 ml/14 fl oz coconut milk
200 ml/7 fl oz chicken stock
1 large red pepper, deseeded and diced
1 green pepper, deseeded and diced
15 g/½ oz coconut chips, toasted or 1 tbsp freshly chopped coriander, to garnish
freshly cooked rice, to serve

### Helpful hint

To make toasted coconut chips, place on a baking sheet and toast in a preheated oven at 200°C/400°F/Gas Mark 6 for 3–5 minutes.

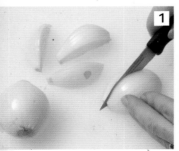

# Chicken & Papaya Curry

1 Heat the oil in a heavy-based saucepan, add the chicken and brown on all sides. Remove and reserve. Add the onions, garlic and ginger to the pan and sauté for 5 minutes. Add the spices and curry paste and cook for 5 minutes, stirring. Return the chicken to the pan and stir until the chicken is coated in the spices.

2 Finely grate the rind from the limes to give 1 tablespoon. Squeeze out the juice to give 3 tablespoons. Stir in the curry leaves, lime rind and juice and stock. Add the coconut milk and carrots and bring to the boil. Reduce the heat, cover and simmer for 30 minutes.

3 Peel the papaya, then remove the seeds and chop the flesh. Add the papaya flesh to the pan with the green pepper and bananas and simmer for a further 15 minutes, or until the chicken is cooked. Spoon into a warmed serving dish and serve with rice and peas.

## Ingredients　　SERVES 4–6

2 tbsp groundnut oil
450 g/1 lb skinless, boneless
　chicken, diced
2 red onions, peeled and cut
　into wedges
4 garlic cloves, peeled and sliced
5 cm/2 inch piece fresh root
　ginger, grated
2 tsp chilli powder
1 tsp ground allspice
1 tbsp mild curry paste
1–2 limes (preferably organic)
few curry leaves
300 ml/$^1/_2$ pint chicken stock
300 ml/$^1/_2$ pint coconut milk
300 g/10 oz carrots, peeled and sliced
1 large papaya (ripe but still firm)
1 green pepper, deseeded
　and chopped
2 small bananas, sliced

### To serve:
freshly cooked rice
freshly cooked peas

# Hot Chicken Drumsticks

1 Discard the skin from the drumsticks, if preferred, and lightly rinse, then pat dry on absorbent kitchen paper. Heat the oil or ghee in a large frying pan, add the fennel seeds and cook for 30 seconds, or until they pop. Add the garlic, onion, ginger, ground coriander and chilli powder and cook gently for 10 minutes, stirring frequently.

2 Push the onion mixture to the side of the pan and add the chicken. Fry the chicken until it is browned on all sides.

3 Add the curry leaves, Hot Pepper Sauce to taste and the chopped tomatoes. Stir in the stock and thyme leaves. Bring to the boil, then reduce the heat, cover and simmer for 20–25 minutes, or until the chicken is cooked. Stir in the chopped spinach and heat for a further 3–4 minutes, or until the spinach has wilted. Serve with new potatoes.

## Ingredients          SERVES 4–6

4–8 chicken drumsticks,
    depending on size
2 tbsp vegetable oil or ghee
1 tsp fennel seeds
4 garlic cloves, peeled and chopped
1 onion, peeled and chopped
5 cm/2 inch piece fresh root ginger,
    peeled and grated
1 tsp ground coriander
1 tsp chilli powder
few curry leaves
1 tbsp hot pepper sauce, or to taste
400 g/14 oz can chopped tomatoes
200 ml/7 fl oz chicken stock
2 tbsp fresh thyme leaves
350 g/12 oz fresh spinach, chopped
freshly cooked new potatoes, to serve

## Tasty tip

The hot pepper sauce could be replaced with Tabasco Sauce, which is also seriously hot. For those who prefer a slightly milder taste use Sweet Chilli Sauce.

# Bengali Chicken Curry

1 Place the chillies, garlic, ginger, shallots, turmeric and 150 ml/¹/₄ pint water in a food processor until smooth, then reserve until required.

2 Lightly rinse the chicken and pat dry with absorbent kitchen paper. Cut the chicken into thin strips, then place in a shallow dish and pour over the spice mixture. Cover and leave to marinate in the refrigerator for 15–30 minutes, stirring occasionally.

3 Heat 2 tablespoons of the oil or ghee in a heavy-based frying pan then using a slotted spoon remove the chicken from the marinade, reserving the marinade. Cook the chicken for 10 minutes, or until sealed.

4 Remove the chicken and reserve. Pour the reserved marinade into the pan and cook gently for 2 minutes. Return the chicken to the pan together with the curry leaves and the remaining water. Bring to the boil, then reduce the heat and simmer for 15 minutes, stirring occasionally, until the chicken is cooked. Spoon into a warmed serving dish, sprinkle with the chopped coriander and serve with bread and salad.

## Ingredients     SERVES 4–6

2–3 red chillies, deseeded
    and chopped
3 garlic cloves, peeled and chopped
5 cm/2 inch piece root ginger,
    peeled and grated
4 shallots, peeled and chopped
1 tsp turmeric
250 ml/8 fl oz water
450 g/1 lb skinless, boneless chicken
2 tbsp vegetable oil or ghee
few curry leaves
1 tbsp freshly chopped coriander

**To serve:**
Indian-style bread
salad

### Tasty tip
This recipe works well with other meats as well as vegetables. If using other meat, ensure that it is thoroughly cooked before serving.

# Creole Chicken Curry

1 Preheat the oven to 190°C/375°F/Gas Mark 5. Place half the garlic in a food processor with the salt, citrus rind and fresh herbs and blend to form a paste.

2 Skin the chicken portions, if preferred, and make small incisions into the flesh. Insert the remaining garlic into the incisions and spread with the prepared herb paste. Place on a plate, cover lightly and leave to marinate in the refrigerator for at least 30 minutes.

3 When ready to cook, heat the oil in a frying pan, add the chicken and brown on all sides. Remove and place in an ovenproof casserole. Add the curry paste with the tamarind paste, Worcestershire sauce and sugar and cook, stirring, for 2 minutes. Add the sweet potato chunks with the juice and stock and bring to the boil. Boil gently, stirring, for 2 minutes, add the curry leaves then pour over the chicken.

4 Cover with a lid and cook in the preheated oven for 30 minutes. Add the sugar snaps and cook for a further 5–8 minutes, or until the chicken is thoroughly cooked. Serve sprinkled with chopped coriander.

## Ingredients    SERVES 4–6

8 garlic cloves, peeled and cut in half
$^1/_2$ tsp salt
1 tbsp grated lime or lemon rind
1 tbsp fresh thyme leaves
1 tbsp fresh oregano leaves
2 tsp freshly chopped coriander
4 chicken thighs
2 tbsp vegetable oil
1 tbsp curry paste
1 tbsp tamarind paste
1 tbsp Worcestershire sauce
2 tsp demerara sugar
350 g/12 oz sweet potatoes, peeled
    and cut into small chunks
250 ml/8 fl oz orange or mango juice
150 ml/$^1/_4$ pint chicken stock
few curry leaves
100 g/4 oz sugar snap peas
2 tbsp freshly chopped coriander,
    to garnish

### Tasty tip

If you can find dried tamarind, soak 75 g/3 oz in 350 ml/12 fl oz water and use in place of the orange juice and stock.

# Tropical Sautéed Chicken Curry

1 Heat the oil in a large frying pan, add the garlic, onions, ginger, chillies and lime rind and fry for 5 minutes, or until beginning to soften.

2 Add the chicken and cook, stirring, until sealed and coated lightly in the garlic and chilli mixture. Add the sugar and curry paste and cook, stirring, for 3 minutes.

3 Pour in the rum and heat for 1 minute. Take off the heat and ignite. When the flames have subsided pour in the stock and coconut milk. Return to the heat, bring to the boil, stirring occasionally, then add the butternut squash.

4 Reduce the heat, cover and simmer for 25 minutes, stirring occasionally. Add the papaya, lime juice and bananas and continue to simmer for 10–15 minutes, or until the chicken and squash are thoroughly cooked. Sprinkle with chopped coriander and serve.

## Ingredients          SERVES 4–6

2 tbsp groundnut oil

4 garlic cloves, peeled and chopped

2 red onions, peeled and cut
    into wedges

5 cm/2 inch piece fresh root ginger,
    peeled and grated

2 green chillies, deseeded and sliced

1 tbsp finely grated lime rind

450 g/1 lb skinless, boneless
    chicken, diced

2 tsp demerara sugar

1 tbsp Madras curry paste

4 tbsp rum

150 ml/$^1/_4$ pint chicken stock

150 ml/$^1/_4$ pint coconut milk

350 g/12 oz butternut squash, peeled,
    deseeded and cut into chunks

1 large or 2 small firm but ripe papaya,
    peeled, deseeded and sliced

3 tbsp lime juice

2 small firm bananas, peeled and cut
    into strips

2 tbsp freshly chopped coriander,
    to garnish

# Spicy Vietnamese Chicken

1   Lightly rinse the chicken portions, pat dry with absorbent kitchen paper and place in a bowl. Add the lemon grass, cinnamon stick and grated ginger, then stir well, cover and leave to chill in the refrigerator for 30 minutes.

2   Heat a wok or large frying pan, add the oil and, when hot, add the chicken and marinade. Cook for 5 minutes, or until browned.

3   Add the garlic, onions and chillies and continue to cook for a further 5 minutes.

4   Add the black pepper, sugar, soy sauce, fish sauce and water and cook for 10 minutes. Add the spring onions and peanuts and cook for 1 minute, then serve immediately with the cooked rice.

## Ingredients   SERVES 4–6

8 small skinless, boneless chicken breasts cut in half, about 350 g/12 oz in weight

2 lemon grass stalks, crushed and outer leaves discarded

1 cinnamon stick, bruised

5 cm/2 inch piece fresh root ginger, peeled and grated

2 tbsp groundnut oil

5 garlic cloves, peeled and sliced

2 red onions, peeled and sliced into wedges

1–2 green chillies, deseeded and chopped

freshly ground black pepper

2 tsp demerara sugar

1 tbsp light soy sauce

1 tbsp fish sauce

6 tbsp water

6 spring onions, trimmed and diagonally sliced

100 g/4 oz roasted peanuts

freshly cooked fragrant rice, to serve

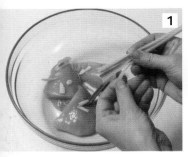

# Stir-fried Chinese Chicken Curry

1   Cut the chicken into small bite-sized pieces and place in a large bowl. Beat the egg white in a separate bowl until fluffy then beat in the salt and cornflour.

2   Pour over the chicken and leave to stand for 15 minutes. Heat a wok or frying pan and when hot, add the oil. Heat for 30 seconds, then drain the chicken and add to the wok or frying pan and cook, stirring, for 2–3 minutes, or until sealed.

3   Remove the chicken and reserve. Add the carrots and peppers to the wok or frying pan and cook, stirring, for 3 minutes, or until the carrots have begun to soften. Stir in the curry paste and cook, stirring, for a further 2 minutes.

4   Add the stock, rice wine or sherry, sugar and soy sauce. Stir well until blended then return the chicken to the pan with the spring onions. Cook for 3–4 minutes, or until the chicken is thoroughly cooked. Serve with the sticky rice.

## Ingredients    SERVES 4–6

350 g/12 oz skinless,
   boneless chicken
1 egg white
1 tsp salt
1 tbsp cornflour
2 tbsp groundnut oil
225 g/8 oz carrots, peeled and cut
   into very thin batons
1 large red pepper, deseeded and cut
   into thin strips
1 large green pepper, deseeded and
   cut into thin strips
1–2 tbsp curry paste
175–200 ml/6–7 fl oz chicken stock
1 tbsp rice wine or dry sherry
1 tsp demerara sugar
1 tbsp light soy sauce
6 spring onions, trimmed and
   diagonally sliced
freshly cooked sticky rice, to serve

### Helpful hint

Marinating the chicken in the egg white and salt helps to tenderise the chicken before cooking.

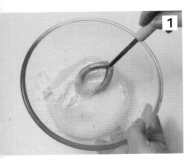

# cken & Chickpea Korma

1  Cut the chicken into small strips and reserve. Heat the oil in a wok or frying pan, add the chicken and cook, stirring, for 3 minutes, or until sealed. Remove and reserve.

2  Add the onion and garlic to the pan and fry gently for 5 minutes, or until the onion has begun to soften. Add the curry paste, garam masala and ground cloves and cook, stirring, for 2 minutes. Return the chicken to the pan and stir well.

3  Add the stock, tomatoes and chickpeas, then bring to the boil, reduce and simmer for 15–20 minutes, or until the chicken is cooked. Stir in the cream. Spoon into a warmed serving dish, sprinkle with the spring onions and serve with Indian-style bread.

## Ingredients       SERVES 4–6

350 g/12 oz skinless,
    boneless chicken
2 tbsp vegetable oil
2 onions, peeled and cut into wedges
2–4 garlic cloves, peeled
    and chopped
2–3 tbsp Korma curry paste
1 tsp garam masala
$^1/_2$–1 tsp ground cloves
450 ml/$^3/_4$ pint chicken stock
225 g/8 oz ripe tomatoes, peeled
    and chopped
400 g/14 oz can chickpeas, drained
    and rinsed
4 tbsp double cream
6 spring onions, trimmed and
    diagonally sliced
Indian-style bread, to serve

### Tasty tip

This is a mild curry, so to make it hotter add either some fresh chillies or chilli powder. Remember to add with the garlic and curry paste.

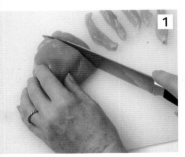

# Tandoori Chicken

1 Lightly rinse the chicken and pat dry with absorbent kitchen paper. Place in a roasting tin and reserve.

2 Blend all the tandoori paste ingredients together and stir until smooth and blended. Pour over the chicken and cover lightly. Leave to marinate in the refrigerator for at least 30 minutes, but longer if time permits.

3 When ready to cook, preheat the oven to 190°C/375°F/Gas Mark 5. Cover the chicken loosely with foil and cook in the oven for 25–30 minutes, or until thoroughly cooked. Remove the foil for the last 5 minutes of the cooking time.

4 Meanwhile, make the dhal. Heat the oil or ghee in a saucepan, add the onion, ginger and spices and fry for 5 minutes, stirring frequently. Stir well then add the lentils and water. Bring to the boil, then reduce the heat, cover and simmer for 25 minutes, or until the lentils are soft. Add more water if necessary during cooking. Garnish the chicken with lemon wedges and serve with the dhal.

## Ingredients     SERVES 4–6

4 skinless, boneless chicken portions, each about 100 g/4 oz in weight
Lemon wedges, to garnish

### For the tandoori paste:
200 ml/7 fl oz natural yogurt
1 tsp hot chilli powder
2 tbsp lemon juice
freshly milled salt
1 tbsp ginger paste or purée
2 garlic cloves, peeled and crushed
1 tsp garam masala

### For the dhal:
2 tbsp vegetable oil or ghee
1 onion, peeled and chopped
5 cm/2 inch piece fresh root ginger, peeled and grated
1 tsp ground coriander
1 tsp ground cumin
pinch each of ground cloves and grated nutmeg
1 tsp turmeric
200 g/7 oz red split lentils
450 ml/³/₄ pint water

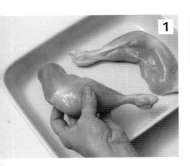

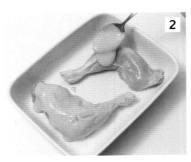

# North Indian Slow-cooked Chicken

**1** Lightly rinse the chicken and pat dry with absorbent kitchen paper. Heat 2 tablespoons of the oil or ghee in a large deep frying pan, add the chicken and brown on all sides. Remove and reserve.

**2** Add a further tablespoon of oil, if necessary, to the pan then add the onions, garlic and half the chillies and fry for 5 minutes, or until beginning to soften. Stir in the curry paste and cook for 2 minutes, stirring frequently. Take care not to burn the mixture.

**3** Take off the heat, return the chicken to the pan and roll around in the paste until lightly coated. Stir in the water. Return to the heat and bring to the boil. Add the curry leaves, then reduce the heat, cover and simmer for 35 minutes, or until the chicken is tender. Pour the lemon juice over the chicken and cook for a further 10 minutes.

**4** Meanwhile, heat the remaining oil in a small frying pan and gently fry the rest of the chillies and the sesame seeds until the chillies have become crisp and the seeds are toasted. Serve the chicken on a bed of rice sprinkled with the crispy chillies and toasted sesame seeds and garnished with coriander sprigs.

## Ingredients    SERVES 4–6

8 small chicken thighs
3–4 tbsp vegetable oil or ghee
2 onions, peeled and cut into wedges
2–3 garlic cloves, peeled and sliced
2 green chillies, deseeded and sliced
2 red chillies, deseeded and sliced
2–3 tbsp Madras curry paste, or
    to taste
450 ml/$^{3}/_{4}$ pint water
few curry leaves
2 tbsp lemon juice
2 tbsp sesame seeds
fresh sprigs coriander, to garnish
freshly  cooked rice, to serve

### Helpful hint

Use a chilli that has a heat tolerance between 3 and 5.

# Chicken with Cashews

1 Lightly rinse the chicken and pat dry with absorbent kitchen paper. Heat the oil in a heavy-based frying pan, add the chicken and brown on all sides, then remove and reserve. Add the halved chillies to the pan and fry for 2 minutes, or until beginning to wilt. Remove and reserve.

2 Add the shallots to the pan and cook, stirring, for 3 minutes. Stir in the curry paste and cook for a further 2 minutes, stirring occasionally. Take off the heat and gradually stir in the stock. Return to the heat and bring to the boil, stirring.

3 Return the chicken to the pan with the pepper strips and the soy sauce. Reduce the heat, cover and simmer for 10 minutes. Add the baby corn and mangetout and continue to cook for 10 minutes, or until the chicken is thoroughly cooked. Spoon into a warmed serving dish and sprinkle with the cashew nuts. Garnish with the reserved chilli halves and serve with freshly cooked rice.

## Ingredients     SERVES 4–6

350 g/12 oz skinless, boneless
   chicken thighs
2 tbsp vegetable oil
1 red chilli, deseeded and cut
   in half lengthways
1 green chilli, deseeded and cut
   in half lengthways
4 shallots, peeled and cut into wedges
1–2 tbsp Thai red curry paste,
   or to taste
300 ml/½ pint chicken stock
1 red pepper, deseeded and cut
   into strips
1 green pepper, deseeded and cut
   into strips
1 tbsp soy sauce
100 g/4 oz baby corn, halved
100 g/4 oz mangetout
50 g/2 oz unsalted shelled cashew
   nuts, roughly chopped
freshly cooked fragrant rice, to serve

### Helpful hint

Make sure you use unsalted cashews –
salted nuts will destroy the flavour.

# Cardamom & Black Pepper Curry

1 Lightly rinse the chicken, pat dry with absorbent kitchen paper and reserve. Crush the cardamom pods and use half of the tiny seeds, which are released, to press into the chicken. Place on a plate, cover loosely and leave to marinate in the refrigerator for at least 30 minutes, longer if time permits.

2 Heat the oil in a heavy-based frying pan, add the chicken and gently brown on all sides. Remove and reserve. Add the onions and garlic to the pan and fry for 5 minutes, or until softened. Sprinkle in the remaining cardamom seeds with the ginger, black pepper and curry paste, stir well and simmer for 5 minutes. Slowly stir in the stock and add the chicken, honey and tomatoes.

3 Bring to the boil, then reduce the heat, cover and simmer for 20 minutes, or until the chicken is thoroughly cooked. Place a chicken breast on each warmed serving plate, add a spoonful of yogurt over each chicken breast and sprinkle with chopped coriander. Serve with freshly cooked noodles.

## Ingredients          SERVES 4–6

4 skinless, boneless chicken breasts, each about 100 g/4 oz in weight
8 cardamom pods
2 tbsp vegetable oil
2 red onions, peeled and sliced
1–2 garlic cloves, peeled and crushed
2.5 cm/1 inch piece fresh root ginger, peeled and grated
1 tsp freshly ground black pepper
1–2 tsp mild curry paste, such as a Korma paste
200 ml/7 fl oz chicken stock
1 tsp clear honey
225 g/8 oz ripe tomatoes, chopped

### To serve:

4 tbsp natural yogurt
1 tbsp freshly chopped coriander
freshly cooked noodles

### Tasty tip

For a change, try using small turkey steaks or even spatchcocked poussin, but cook for longer, at least 40 minutes.

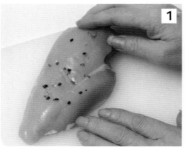

# Turkey Curry

1 Heat the oil or ghee in a large frying pan, add the seeds and fry for 30 seconds, or until they pop. Add the onions, garlic and chillies and continue to fry, stirring frequently, for 5 minutes.

2 Sprinkle in the turmeric and ground coriander and cook for 2 minutes. Add the turkey strips and cook for a further 5 minutes, or until the turkey is sealed and coated in the spices.

3 Trim and cut the aubergines in half then add to the pan.

4 Blend the tomato purée with the water and gradually stir into the pan. Bring to the boil, then reduce the heat, cover and simmer for 15 minutes.

5 Add the courgettes and continue to simmer for a further 10 minutes, or until the turkey is tender. Add the sliced mango and heat for 2 minutes until hot. Sprinkle with chopped coriander and serve with freshly cooked rice.

## Ingredients                SERVES 4–6

2 tbsp vegetable oil or ghee
1 tsp fennel seeds
1 tsp cumin seeds
1 tsp fenugreek seeds
2 red onions, peeled and cut into
    half-moon slices
2–3 garlic cloves, peeled and sliced
2 green chillies, deseeded and sliced
1 tsp turmeric
1 tsp ground coriander
350 g/12 oz fresh turkey breast
    steaks, sliced into strips
225 g/8 oz baby aubergines
2 tbsp tomato purée
450 ml/³/₄ pint water
300 g/10 oz courgettes,
    trimmed and sliced
1 ripe mango, peeled, stoned
    and sliced
2 tbsp freshly chopped coriander,
    to garnish
freshly cooked basmati rice, to serve

# Thai Green Turkey Curry

1  Place the aubergines into a colander and sprinkle with the salt. Set over a plate or in the sink to drain and leave for 30 minutes. Rinse under cold running water and pat dry on absorbent kitchen paper.

2  Heat a wok or large frying pan, add the oil and, when hot, add the shallots and garlic and stir-fry for 3 minutes, or until beginning to brown. Add the curry paste and stir-fry for 1–2 minutes. Pour in the stock, fish sauce and lemon juice and simmer for 10 minutes.

3  Add the turkey, red pepper and French beans to the wok with the aubergines. Return to the boil, then simmer for 10–15 minutes, or until the turkey and vegetables are tender. Add the creamed coconut and stir until melted and the sauce has thickened. Turn into a warmed serving dish and serve immediately with rice.

## Ingredients    SERVES 4

4 baby aubergines, trimmed
  and quartered
1 tsp salt
2 tbsp groundnut oil
4 shallots, peeled and halved, or
  quartered if large
2 garlic cloves, peeled and sliced
2 tbsp Thai green curry paste
150 ml/$^1/_4$ pint chicken stock
1 tbsp Thai fish sauce
1 tbsp lemon juice
350 g/12 oz boneless, skinless turkey
  breast, cubed
1 red pepper, deseeded and sliced
125 g/4 oz French beans, trimmed
  and halved
25 g/1 oz creamed coconut
freshly cooked Thai fragrant rice,
  to serve

### Food fact

Several types of aubergine are grown in Thailand. Generally the Thais prefer the small thin varieties, which have a more delicate flavour. If you are unable to find them, use baby aubergines.

# Duck & Orange Curry

1 Lightly rinse the duck breasts, pat dry with absorbent kitchen paper, then slice thinly and reserve. Heat the oil or ghee in a deep frying pan, add the fenugreek seeds and fry for 30 seconds, or until they pop.

2 Add the ginger, onions, garlic and chillies and cook, stirring, for 5 minutes, or until the onions have begun to soften. Using a slotted spoon, remove from the pan and reserve. Deseed the red pepper and slice. Reserve until required.

3 Add the duck strips to the pan and cook, stirring, for 5–8 minutes, or until sealed. Return the spice mixture to the pan with the curry paste and stir well until the duck strips are coated in the spices. Pour in the stock and coconut milk and bring to the boil. Grate the rind from the orange and add to the pan, then reduce the heat, cover and simmer for 10 minutes.

4 Peel the orange and divide the flesh into small segments. Stir into the pan with the curry leaves, red pepper slices and courgettes. Continue to cook for 10–12 minutes, or until the duck and vegetables are tender. Serve with freshly cooked rice.

## Ingredients     SERVES 4–6

350 g/12 oz skinless, boneless
    duck breasts
2 tbsp vegetable oil or ghee
1 tsp fenugreek seeds
5 cm/2 inch piece fresh root ginger,
    peeled and grated
2 red onions, peeled and sliced
4 garlic cloves, peeled and sliced
1 red chilli, deseeded and chopped
1 green chilli, deseeded and chopped
1 large red pepper
1 tbsp Madras curry paste, or to taste
200 ml/7 fl oz chicken stock
300 ml/$^1$/$_2$ pint coconut milk
1 large orange
few curry leaves
2 courgettes, trimmed and sliced
freshly cooked white and wild rice,
    to serve

### Tasty tip

Sweet red or yellow plums work very well with this recipe as well as the orange.

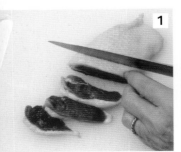

# Fish & Seafood

Looking for something different to cook tonight? Fish and seafood curries are so full of exotic flavours and different textures that a great dinner cannot be far away! Grilled Sea Bass with Tomato Curry Sauce and Aromatic Seafood Singapore Curry are just two delicious ideas for a scrumptious meal. Do not forget the health benefits of fish too!

# Coconut Fish Curry

1  Put 1 tablespoon of the oil into a large frying pan and cook the onion, pepper and garlic for 5 minutes, or until soft. Add the remaining oil, curry paste, ginger and chilli and cook for a further minute.

2  Pour in the coconut milk and bring to the boil, reduce the heat and simmer gently for 5 minutes, stirring occasionally. Add the fish to the pan and continue to simmer gently for 5–10 minutes, or until the fish is tender, but not overcooked.

3  Meanwhile, cook the rice in a saucepan of boiling salted water for 15 minutes, or until tender. Drain the rice thoroughly and turn out into a serving dish.

4  Stir the chopped coriander and chutney gently into the fish curry and season to taste with salt and pepper. Spoon the fish curry over the cooked rice, garnish with lime wedges and coriander sprigs and serve immediately with spoonfuls of Greek yogurt and warm naan bread.

## Ingredients                    SERVES 4

2 tbsp groundnut oil
1 medium onion, peeled and
    very finely chopped
1 yellow pepper, deseeded and
    finely chopped
1 garlic clove, peeled and crushed
1 tbsp mild curry paste
2.5 cm/1 inch piece of root ginger,
    peeled and grated
1 red chilli, deseeded and finely chopped
400 ml/14 oz can coconut milk
700 g/1½ lb white fish, such as monkfish
    fillets, skinned and cut into chunks
225 g/8 oz basmati rice
1 tbsp freshly chopped coriander
1 tbsp mango chutney
salt and freshly ground black pepper

### To garnish:
lime wedges
fresh coriander sprigs

### To serve:
Greek yogurt
warm naan bread

# Salmon Parcels

1 Preheat the oven to 180°C/350°F/Gas Mark 4. Cut out 4 x 20.5 cm/8 inch squares of nonstick baking paper or foil. Lightly rinse the salmon and pat dry with absorbent kitchen paper. Place a salmon fillet on each square of paper.

2 Sprinkle the fillets equally with the ginger, chillies and garlic. Blend the curry paste with the sweet chilli sauce and pour 1 tablespoon of the mixture over each salmon fillet. Top with sprigs of fresh coriander.

3 Fold the paper to completely encase the fillets and all the flavourings. Place in roasting tin or on a baking tray and cook in the preheated oven for 20 minutes.

4 Place a parcel on each warmed dinner plate and let each person open up the parcels, so they can enjoy the pleasure of the spicy aroma. Serve with lime wedges, new potatoes and steamed vegetables.

## Ingredients    SERVES 4–6

4 salmon fillets, each about 150 g/
   5 oz in weight
5 cm/2 inch piece fresh root ginger,
   peeled and grated
1 red chilli, deseeded and sliced
1 green chilli, deseeded and sliced
2–3 garlic cloves, peeled and crushed
1 tbsp curry paste
4 tbsp sweet chilli sauce
few sprigs of fresh coriander

**To serve:**
lime wedges
new potatoes
steamed vegetables

**Helpful hint**
Other fish can also be cooked in this manner.

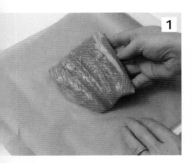

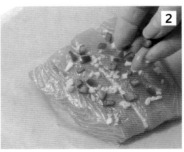

# Salmon & Mango Curry

1 Lightly rinse the salmon fillets and discard any pin bones, if necessary. Place in a shallow dish and reserve.

2 Heat the oil in a frying pan, add the chilli, garlic and onions and fry for 3 minutes. Add the spices and cook, stirring, for 2 minutes. Remove from the heat, cool slightly, then remove half the spice mixture and use to spread over the top of the salmon. Cover lightly and leave in the refrigerator for 15 minutes.

3 Add the sugar and tomatoes to the spices remaining in the pan. Half-fill the empty tomato can with water, swirl to remove any remaining pieces of tomato and add to the pan.

4 Bring the sauce to the boil, then reduce the heat, cover and simmer for 5–7 minutes, or until cooked, stirring occasionally. Carefully add the fillets to the frying pan. Stir in the chutney. Bring to the boil, then reduce the heat and simmer gently for 5 minutes.

5 Meanwhile, peel the mango and discard the stone. Chop the flesh and add to the pan. Add Hot Pepper Sauce to taste and continue to simmer for 3–5 minutes, or until the fish is tender. Sprinkle with chopped parsley and serve with cooked rice.

## Ingredients  SERVES 4–6

4 salmon fillets, each about 150 g/5 oz
    in weight
2 tbsp vegetable oil
$^{1}/_{2}$–1 Scotch bonnet yellow chilli,
    deseeded and chopped
4 garlic cloves, peeled and chopped
2 medium onions, peeled
    and chopped
$1^{1}/_{2}$ tsp ground allspice
1 tsp ground cloves
1 tsp ground cinnamon stick
1 tsp demerara sugar
400 g/14 oz can chopped tomatoes
2 tbsp mango chutney (see page 180)
1 large fresh ripe mango
1 tsp hot pepper sauce, or to taste
2 tbsp freshly chopped
    flat-leaf parsley
freshly cooked white and wild rice,
    to serve

### Helpful hint

If fresh mango is unavailable, try using canned mango or even a papaya.

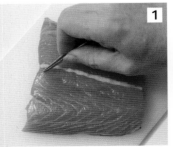

# Fish & Aubergine Curry

1 Heat 1 tablespoon of the oil in a saucepan or frying pan, add the onions and garlic and cook, stirring, for 2 minutes. Add the curry paste and continue to cook for a further 3 minutes. Cut the aubergines into quarters.

2 Add the aubergines to the pan with the tomatoes. Stir until coated in the curry paste. Blend the tomato purée with 4 tablespoons of the stock and stir into the pan. Add the remaining stock and bring to the boil. Reduce the heat and simmer for 12–15 minutes, stirring occasionally, to form a thick sauce. Stir in 1 tablespoon of the chopped coriander.

3 Meanwhile, line a grill rack with foil and preheat the grill. Lightly rinse the fish fillets and pat dry with absorbent kitchen paper. Brush the fillets with the remaining oil and sprinkle with the grated lime rind, black pepper and chopped chilli.

4 Cook under the grill for 5–8 minutes, or until cooked. Place 2 fillets on a warmed plate, one on top of the other and sprinkle over the lime juice. Spoon over some of the prepared curry sauce and sprinkle with chopped coriander. Serve the remaining sauce separately with dhal and salad.

## Ingredients    SERVES 4–6

2 tbsp vegetable oil
2 medium onions, peeled and chopped
2 garlic cloves, peeled and chopped
2 tbsp Madras curry paste
300 g/10 oz baby aubergines
300 g/10 oz fresh ripe
    tomatoes, chopped
1 tbsp tomato purée
200 ml/7 fl oz vegetable stock
1 tbsp freshly chopped coriander
8 small sea bass fillets
grated rind and juice 2 limes
freshly ground black pepper
1 red chilli, deseeded and chopped

**To serve:**
freshly cooked dhal
    (*see* pages 104, 198 and 200)
salad

**Tasty tip**
The fish can be cooked in a frying pan. Heat the oil in the pan rather than brushing over the fish. Sprinkle with the other ingredients and fry for 5–8 minutes.

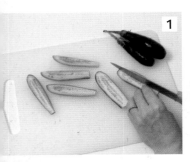

# Fish & Okra Curry

1 Place the saffron strands in a small bowl and cover with hot but not boiling water. Leave for at least 10 minutes. Skin the fish fillets, if necessary, and remove any pin bones. Cut into small chunks and reserve.

2 Heat the oil in a large frying pan, add the seeds and cook for 30 seconds, or until they pop. Add the cinnamon stick and cardamom pods and cook for 30 seconds before adding the garlic, onion, ground coriander and chilli powder.

3 Cook for 2 minutes, stirring, then add the chopped tomatoes and stock. Bring to the boil, then reduce the heat and simmer for 10 minutes.

4 Add the fish to the pan with the okra and continue to cook for 5–8 minutes, or until the fish is tender and the okra is cooked. Add black pepper to taste. Serve garnished with the lemon wedges and warm bread.

## Ingredients        SERVES 4–6

few saffron strands
450 g/1 lb fish fillets, such as haddock
    or salmon
2 tbsp vegetable oil
1 tsp fenugreek seeds
1 tsp cumin seeds
small piece cinnamon stick, bruised
4 green cardamom pods, cracked
2 garlic cloves, peeled and chopped
1 medium onion, peeled and chopped
1 tsp ground coriander
1 tsp chilli powder
4 medium tomatoes, chopped
300 ml/$^1/_2$ pint vegetable or fish stock
225 g/8 oz okra, trimmed and
    sliced diagonally
freshly ground black pepper
lemon wedges, to garnish
warm Indian-style bread, to serve

## Food fact
Okra is also referred to as 'ladies' fingers'.

# Grilled Sea Bass with Tomato Curry

1. Mix the chopped garlic, shallots and chillies together and divide into 2 portions. Lightly rinse the fish fillets and sprinkle with one portion of the garlic and chilli mixture. Leave in the refrigerator until ready to cook.

2. Heat 2 tablespoons of the oil in a saucepan, add the remaining portion of the garlic and chilli mixture and the sliced celery and fry for 3 minutes. Add the cloves, star anise, cinnamon stick and lemon grass and cook gently for 5 minutes, stirring frequently.

3. Blend the tomato purée with the water and add to the pan with the chopped tomatoes. Bring to the boil, then reduce the heat, cover and simmer for 10–12 minutes, or until a thick sauce is formed. If liked, remove the whole spices and pass through a food processor to form a smooth sauce. Stir in the cream and heat gently when required.

4. Line the grill rack with foil and preheat the grill to medium-high. Place the fish fillets on the foil and drizzle with the remaining oil. Cook for 8–10 minutes, or until cooked. Garnish with lime wedges and serve with the prepared sauce and Curried Potatoes with Spinach.

## Ingredients    SERVES 4–6

4 garlic cloves, peeled and chopped

3 shallots, peeled and finely chopped

1–2 red chillies, deseeded and
  finely chopped

4–8 sea bass, depending on
  size, filleted

3 tbsp vegetable oil

1 celery stick, trimmed and finely sliced

2 whole cloves

3 star anise

1 small cinnamon stick, lightly bruised

1 lemon grass stalk, bruised and outer
  leaves discarded

1 tbsp tomato purée

4 tbsp water

300 g/10 oz ripe tomatoes, peeled
  and chopped

4 tbsp double cream

lime wedges, to garnish

Curried Potatoes with Spinach
  (see page 186)

### Helpful hint

Use a can of chopped tomatoes in place of the fresh tomatoes, if preferred.

# Curried Fish Caribbean-style

1  Preheat the oven to 180°C/350°F/Gas Mark 4. Lightly rinse the fish fillets and place in a lightly oiled shallow ovenproof dish. Sprinkle with a little salt and drizzle over the lime juice. Cover and leave in the refrigerator for 10 minutes while making the sauce.

2  Heat the oil in a saucepan, add the garlic and onion and fry for 3 minutes. Add the tomatoes, spices, herbs, hot pepper sauce, to taste, and the water. Bring to the boil, then reduce the heat and simmer, stirring, for 10 minutes, or until slightly reduced.

3  Spoon the sauce over the fish fillets, cover with foil and cook in the preheated oven for 15 minutes. Remove the foil and cook for a further 5 minutes, or until the fish is tender. Serve sprinkled with spring onions (if using), with freshly cooked vegetables.

## Ingredients          SERVES 4–6

4 fish steaks, such as cod, salmon
    or tuna, each about 150 g/5 oz
    in weight
freshly milled rock salt, to sprinkle
4 tbsp lime juice
2 tbsp groundnut oil
3 garlic cloves, peeled and chopped
1 onion, peeled and chopped
225 g/8 oz tomatoes, peeled
    and chopped
1 tsp turmeric
$1/2$ tsp chilli powder, or to taste
1 tsp ground allspice
1 tsp dried thyme
1 tsp dried oregano
1 tbsp freshly chopped coriander
1–3 tsp hot pepper sauce, to taste
150 ml/$1/4$ pint water
4 spring onions, trimmed and
    chopped, to garnish (optional)
freshly cooked vegetables, to serve

### Helpful hint

Do not leave the fish too long after sprinkling with the salt and lime juice.

# Malaysian Fish Curry

1 Preheat the oven to 180°C/350°F/Gas Mark 4. Lightly rinse the fish fillets and pat dry with absorbent kitchen paper. Place in a lightly oiled ovenproof dish.

2 Heat the oil in a frying pan, add the garlic and ginger and fry for 2 minutes. Add the turmeric, ground coriander and curry paste and cook for a further 3 minutes, stirring frequently. Take off the heat and gradually stir in the coconut milk. Cool slightly then pour over the fish.

3 Cover with lightly buttered foil and cook in the preheated oven for 20 minutes, or until the fish is tender. Sprinkle with chopped coriander then garnish with lime wedges, if using, and serve with stir-fried vegetables and freshly cooked rice.

## Ingredients          SERVES 4–6

4 firm fish fillets, such as salmon, haddock or pollack, each about 150 g/5 oz in weight
1 tbsp groundnut oil
2 garlic cloves, peeled and crushed
2.5 cm/1 inch piece fresh root ginger, peeled and grated
1 tsp turmeric
1 tsp ground coriander
2 tbsp Madras curry paste
300 ml/½ pint coconut milk
2 tbsp freshly chopped coriander
lime wedges, to garnish (optional)
stir-fried Oriental vegetables and fragrant rice, to serve

### Helpful hint
Use a mild or medium heat curry paste – a really hot curry paste will destroy the delicate taste of the fish.

# Spicy Sardines

1 Lightly rinse the sardines and pat dry with absorbent kitchen paper. Make diagonal slashes across both sides of the sardines and reserve.

2 Blend the lime juice, ginger, garlic, ground coriander, cumin and curry paste together.

3 Lightly smear the mixture over the fish. Leave in the refrigerator until required.

4 Heat the oil in a large nonstick frying pan, add the sardines, in batches depending on size, and cook for 2–4 minutes on each side. Remove, garnish with the lime wedges and serve with Tarka Dhal and a green salad.

## Ingredients  SERVES 4–6

8–12 fresh sardines, depending on size
2 tbsp lime juice
2.5 cm/1 inch piece fresh root ginger, peeled and grated
3 garlic cloves, peeled and crushed
1 tsp ground coriander
1 tsp ground cumin
1 tbsp Madras curry paste
2–3 tbsp vegetable oil
lime wedges, to garnish

### To serve:

Tarka Dhal (see page 200)
green salad

### Tasty tip

If liked, the sardines can be grilled. Place on a foil-lined grill rack and cook under a preheated medium-hot grill for 6–8 minutes, or until cooked.

# Bombay Tuna Patties

1  Lightly oil a nonstick frying pan with about 2 teaspoons of oil and gently cook the tuna fish for 2–3 minutes on each side, or until just cooked. Remove and leave until cool enough to handle. Chop roughly and place in a mixing bowl.

2  Cook the potatoes in a saucepan of boiling water for 12–15 minutes, or until tender. Drain and mash into a chunky mash.

3  Add to the tuna together with the turmeric and mix lightly together. Heat the remaining oil in the frying pan, add the seeds and fry for 30 seconds, or until they pop. Add the remaining spices and continue to fry gently for 2 minutes, stirring constantly. Remove and stir into the tuna mixture and mix well.

4  Using damp hands, shape the tuna mixture into 8–12 small rounds and place on a plate. Blend the cornflour with the water to form a coating batter. Place the breadcrumbs on a plate.

5  Heat the oil for deep-frying in a deep large saucepan or wok to a temperature of 180°C/350°F. Dip the tuna patties into the cornflour and then in the breadcrumbs. Deep-fry, in batches, for 2–3 minutes, or until golden and crisp. Drain on absorbent kitchen paper. Repeat until all the patties are cooked. Serve with salad, tomato chutney and/or Raita.

## Ingredients    SERVES 4–6

2 tbsp vegetable oil, plus extra for deep-frying
300 g/10 oz fresh tuna steaks
225 g/8 oz potatoes, peeled and cut into small chunks
$^{1}/_{2}$ tsp turmeric
1 tsp cumin seeds
1 tsp fenugreek seeds
1 tsp ground coriander
1 tsp garam masala
few curry leaves
1 tsp ginger purée
$^{1}/_{2}$–1 tsp chilli powder, or to taste
75 g/3 oz cornflour
about 50–85 ml/2–3 fl oz water
75 g/3 oz dried breadcrumbs

### To serve:

tomato chutney, raita (*see* page 182) or fresh salad

### Helpful hint

Fresh breadcrumbs are better than shop-bought. Dry fresh breadcrumbs in a hot oven until they separate.

# Aromatic Sole

1 Cook the rice in a saucepan of boiling water for 12 minutes, or until cooked. Drain and reserve. Rinse the fish fillets and pat dry with absorbent kitchen paper, and cut into strips. Reserve.

2 Heat 1 tablespoon of the oil in a nonstick frying pan, add the cumin and sesame seeds and fry for 30 seconds, or until they pop. Drain on absorbent kitchen paper and reserve.

3 Heat a further tablespoon of oil in a wok or large saucepan, add the lemon grass, cinnamon stick, cardamom pods, cloves, curry leaves and grated ginger and gently stir-fry for 2 minutes. Add the curry paste and continue to cook gently for 2 minutes, stirring constantly. Take off the heat and gradually stir in the coconut milk. Half-fill the coconut milk can with water, then swirl to dislodge any coconut milk on the sides of the can and add to the pan. Bring to the boil, then reduce the heat and simmer for 10 minutes.

4 Heat the remaining oil in a small saucepan, add the mushrooms and cook for 2 minutes. Drain and add to the sauce with the sole. Continue to simmer for 5–8 minutes, or until the fish is tender. Spoon the rice into warmed serving dishes and ladle over the sole and coconut milk. Sprinkle with a few seeds and serve.

## Ingredients      SERVES 4–6

175 g/6 oz Thai fragrant rice

8 sole fillets, about 350 g/12 oz total weight, skinned

3 tbsp groundnut oil

1 tsp cumin seeds

1 tsp sesame seeds

1 lemon grass stalk, bruised and outer leaves discarded

1 small cinnamon stick, bruised

4 cardamom pods, cracked

2 whole cloves

2–3 curry leaves

2.5 cm/1 inch piece fresh root ginger, peeled and grated

1 tbsp Madras curry paste

400 ml/14 fl oz can coconut milk

100 g/4 oz button mushrooms, wiped and sliced

## Helpful hint

Plaice can be used instead of the sole as could squid, prawns or mussels.

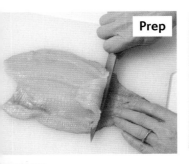

Prep

1

2

# Red Prawn Curry with Jasmine-scented rice

1 Using a pestle and mortar or a spice grinder, grind the coriander and cumin seeds, peppercorns and salt to a fine powder. Add the dried chillies one at a time and grind to a fine powder.

2 Place the shallots, garlic, galangal or ginger, one kaffir lime leaf or rind, chilli powder and shrimp paste in a food processor. Add the ground spices and process until a thick paste forms. Scrape down the bowl once or twice, adding a few drops of water if the mixture is too thick and not forming a paste. Stir in the lemon grass.

3 Transfer the paste to a large wok and cook over a medium heat for 2–3 minutes or until fragrant.

4 Stir in the coconut milk, bring to the boil, then lower the heat and simmer for about 10 minutes. Add the chilli, fish sauce, sugar and red pepper and simmer for 15 minutes.

5 Stir in the prawns and cook for 5 minutes, or until the prawns are pink and tender. Shred the remaining kaffir lime leaves and add to the prawns with the remaining herbs. Heat for a further minute and serve immediately with the cooked rice.

## Ingredients SERVES 4

2 tsp coriander seeds; 1 tsp cumin seeds; 1 tsp black peppercorns; $\frac{1}{2}$ tsp salt; 1–2 dried red chillies; 2 shallots, peeled and chopped; 3–4 garlic cloves; 2.5 cm/1 inch piece fresh galangal or root ginger, peeled and chopped; 1 dried or fresh kaffir lime leaf or 1 tsp lime rind; $\frac{1}{2}$ tsp red chilli powder; $\frac{1}{2}$ tbsp shrimp paste; 1–1$\frac{1}{2}$ lemon grass stalks, thinly sliced and outer leaves removed; 750 ml/1$\frac{1}{4}$ pints coconut milk; 1 red chilli, deseeded and thinly sliced; 2 tbsp Thai fish sauce; 2 tsp soft brown sugar; 1 red pepper, deseeded and thinly sliced; 550 g/1$\frac{1}{4}$ lb large peeled tiger prawns; 2 fresh kaffir lime leaves, shredded (optional); 2 tbsp fresh mint leaves, shredded; 2 tbsp Thai or Italian basil leaves, shredded; freshly cooked Thai fragrant rice, to serve

# Lobster & Prawn Curry

1 Using a sharp knife, slice the lobster meat thickly. Wash the tiger prawns and pat dry with absorbent kitchen paper. Make a small 1 cm/½ inch cut at the tail end of each prawn and reserve.

2 Heat a large wok, then add the oil and, when hot, stir-fry the lobster and tiger prawns for 4–6 minutes, or until pink. Using a slotted spoon, transfer to a plate and keep warm in a low oven.

3 Add the spring onions and stir-fry for 2 minutes, then stir in the garlic and ginger and stir-fry for a further 2 minutes. Add the curry paste and stir-fry for 1 minute.

4 Pour in the coconut cream, lime rind and juice and the seasoning. Bring to the boil and simmer for 1 minute. Return the prawns and lobster and any juices to the wok and simmer for 2 minutes. Stir in two thirds of the freshly chopped coriander to the wok mixture, then sprinkle with the remaining coriander and serve immediately.

## Ingredients        SERVES 4

225 g/8 oz cooked lobster meat,
   shelled if necessary
225 g/8 oz raw tiger prawns, peeled
   and deveined
2 tbsp groundnut oil
2 bunches spring onions, trimmed
   and thickly sliced
2 garlic cloves, peeled and chopped
2.5 cm/1 inch piece fresh root
   ginger, peeled and cut
   into matchsticks
2 tbsp Thai red curry paste
200 ml/7 fl oz coconut cream
grated rind and juice of 1 lime
salt and freshly ground black pepper
3 tbsp freshly chopped coriander
freshly cooked Thai fragrant rice,
   to serve

### Food fact

This dish is not as expensive as it first appears, since 1 small lobster is easily enough for 4 people. If fresh lobster is unavailable, use monkfish cut into slices.

# Curried Prawn Kebabs

1 Heat the oil in a wok or frying pan, add the seeds and fry for 30 seconds, or until they pop. Add the turmeric, chilli powder, ground coriander, chopped chilli and grated ginger and fry over a gentle heat for 2 minutes. Stir in the lime juice and cook, stirring, for 30 seconds. Remove from the heat and cool slightly before stirring in the yogurt.

2 Rinse the prawns and pat dry with absorbent kitchen paper, then place in a shallow dish large enough for the prawns to lie in a single layer. Pour the spicy yogurt over the prawns, cover lightly and leave to marinate in the refrigerator for at least 30 minutes, turning the prawns over a couple of times.

3 Line a grill rack with foil and preheat the grill, or light the barbecue. Drain the prawns, reserving the marinade, and thread them with the lime wedges onto the drained kebab skewers. Place on the grill rack or barbecue rack and cook for 5–10 minutes, or until cooked, turning the prawns over occasionally and brushing with a little of the reserved marinade. Turn the heat down if the prawns under the grill are cooking too quickly and beginning to burn. Serve with salad and bread.

## Ingredients SERVES 4–6

1 tbsp vegetable oil
1 tsp fennel seeds
1 tsp cumin seeds
1 tsp turmeric
1 tsp chilli powder
1 tsp ground coriander
1 red chilli, deseeded and chopped
5 cm/2 inch piece fresh root ginger,
   peeled and grated
2 tbsp lime juice
300 ml/$^1/_2$ pint natural yogurt
350 g/12 oz raw large prawns, peeled
2–3 limes, cut into wedges
salad and Indian-style bread,
   to serve
4–8 wooden kebab skewers, soaked
   in cold water for 30 minutes

### Tasty tip

If liked, thread a few pieces of red and yellow pepper with the prawns.

# Singapore-style Curry

1 Cook the rice in a saucepan of boiling water for 12–15 minutes, or until tender. Drain and keep warm. Clean the prawns, removing the thin black thread if necessary, and reserve. Heat the oil in a large pan or wok, add the ginger and chillies and fry for 1 minute.

2 Add the shallots and red pepper and stir-fry for 3 minutes. Add the courgette, sweet chilli sauce to taste and chopped tomatoes and simmer for 2 minutes.

3 Add the prawns and continue to simmer for 5 minutes, or until the prawns have turned pink.

4 Place a portion of cooked rice in the base of 4 deep serving bowls and spoon over some of the prawn mixture and liquor. Sprinkle each with chopped coriander and serve.

## Ingredients    SERVES 4–6

175 g/6 oz basmati rice

450 g/1 lb large prawns, peeled

2 tbsp vegetable oil

5 cm/2 inch piece fresh root ginger, peeled and grated

1–3 bird's eye red chillies, deseeded and sliced

4 shallots, peeled and cut into thin wedges

1 red pepper, deseeded and cut into small chunks

1 large courgette, trimmed and cut into chunks

2–4 tbsp sweet chilli sauce

225 g/8 oz ripe tomatoes, peeled and chopped

2 tbsp freshly chopped coriander

## Helpful hint

Any seafood can be cooked in this way, just increase the cooking time according to the fish used.

# Spicy-battered Seafood

1 Peel the prawns and remove the thin black vein, if necessary. Rinse lightly and dry with absorbent kitchen paper. Clean the squid, if necessary, rinse and if tiny leave whole or cut into thick strips or rings. Leave to dry on absorbent kitchen paper. Mix the cornflour and curry powder together, then use to coat the prawns and squid. Reserve.

2 For the batter, sift the flour, curry powder and turmeric into a mixing bowl and make a well in the centre. Gradually beat in the water, beating well to form a smooth batter. Beat well to ensure there are no lumps.

3 Heat the oil for deep-frying in a deep-fryer or large deep saucepan to a temperature of 180°C/350°F. Dip the cornflour-coated seafood into the batter allowing any excess to drip back into the bowl and deep-fry 2–4 pieces of seafood for 3–4 minutes, or until golden brown and crisp. Remove and drain on absorbent kitchen paper. Repeat until all the seafood is cooked. Serve garnished with lime wedges and a spicy tomato dip and warm pitta bread.

### Ingredients   SERVES 4–6
350 g/12 oz large raw prawns
175 g/6 oz baby squid
50 g/2 oz cornflour
1 tbsp curry powder
vegetable oil, for deep-frying
lime wedges, to garnish

### For the batter:
100 g/4 oz white self-raising flour
1 tsp curry powder
$\frac{1}{2}$ tsp turmeric
175–200 ml/6–7 fl oz water

### To serve:
spicy tomato dip
strips of warm pitta bread

### Helpful hint
If you do not have a thermometer to test the temperature, drop a small cube of bread into the hot oil; if it turns crisp and golden in 30 seconds the oil is ready.

# Thai Curried Seafood

1 Heat a wok or large frying pan, add 1 tablespoon of the oil and, when hot, add the scallops and stir-fry for 2 minutes or until opaque and firm. Transfer to a plate with any juices.

2 Heat the remaining oil. Add the onion, garlic, ginger and chillies and stir-fry for 1 minute or until they begin to soften.

3 Add the curry paste, coriander, cumin and lemon grass and stir-fry for 2 minutes. Add the tomatoes and stock, bring to the boil then simmer for 5 minutes or until reduced, stirring constantly. Stir in the coconut milk and simmer for 2 minutes.

4 Stir in the mussels, cover and simmer for 2 minutes or until they begin to open. Stir in the prawns, crab meat and reserved scallops with any juices and cook for 2 minutes or until heated through. Discard the lemon grass and any unopened mussels. Stir in the chopped coriander. Tip into a large warmed serving dish and garnish with the coconut, if using. Serve immediately with rice or noodles.

## Ingredients  SERVES 6–8

2 tbsp groundnut oil

450 g/1 lb scallops, with coral attached if preferred, halved if large

1 onion, peeled and finely chopped

4 garlic cloves, peeled and finely chopped

5 cm/2 inch piece fresh root ginger, peeled and finely chopped

1–2 red chillies, deseeded and thinly sliced

1–2 tbsp curry paste (heat to taste)

1 tsp ground coriander

1 tsp ground cumin

1 lemon grass stalk, bruised

225 g/8 oz can chopped tomatoes

125 ml/4 fl oz chicken stock or water

450 ml/³/₄ pint coconut milk

12 live mussels, scrubbed and beards removed

450 g/1 lb cooked peeled prawns

225 g/8 oz frozen or canned crab meat, drained

2 tbsp freshly chopped coriander

freshly shredded coconut, to garnish (optional)

freshly cooked rice or noodles, to serve

# Goan Seafood Curry

1 Prepare the seafood by removing any skin or bones from the monkfish and salmon then cut into small chunks. Clean the scallops, if necessary and cut in half, if large. Peel the prawns and discard the heads. Remove the black vein, if necessary. Cut the squid into rings, then rinse and pat dry with absorbent kitchen paper. Reserve.

2 Place the coconut, fenugreek and cumin seeds in a food processor or grinder with the ground coriander, ginger, chilli, turmeric and black pepper. Add 6 tablespoons of water and blend to a paste.

3 Heat the oil in a deep frying pan, add the onion and gently fry for 10 minutes, or until softened. Add the spice paste and continue to fry for a further 5 minutes, adding a little water if beginning to stick to the pan.

4 Add the fish, coconut milk, tomatoes and the remaining 2 tablespoons of water, stir gently then simmer for 10–12 minutes, or until the fish is cooked. Serve with freshly cooked rice.

## Ingredients SERVES 4–6

550 g/1 lb 4 oz mixed seafood, such as monkfish fillets, salmon, scallops, large prawns and squid
100 g/4 oz desiccated coconut
1 tsp fenugreek seeds
1 tsp cumin seeds
1 tsp ground coriander
small piece fresh root ginger, peeled and grated
1 small red chilli, deseeded and sliced
1 tsp turmeric
$^1/_2$ tsp freshly ground black pepper
8 tbsp water
1 tbsp vegetable oil
1 medium onion, peeled and cut into thin rings
350 ml/12 fl oz coconut milk
225 g/8 oz tomatoes, peeled and chopped
freshly cooked rice, to serve

### Tasty tip

If you prefer a hotter and spicier curry, stir in 1–2 deseeded and sliced chillies at the end of cooking.

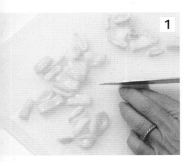

# Seafood in Green Curry Sauce

1 Remove any pin bones if necessary from the fish and cut into small chunks; reserve.

2 Heat the oil in a wok or large saucepan, add the onion and fry for 2 minutes, stirring frequently. Add the ginger, lemon grass, lime leaves and chopped chilli and continue to stir-fry for 3 minutes.

3 Add the green curry paste and soy sauce, stir well then add the coconut milk and water. Bring to the boil, then reduce the heat and simmer for 5 minutes.

4 Add the fish and continue to simmer for 12–15 minutes, or until the fish is cooked. Add the lime juice, stir in the chopped coriander and serve with the freshly cooked fragrant rice.

## Ingredients      SERVES 4

175 g/6 oz cod or haddock
   fillet, skinned
175 g/6 oz salmon fillet, skinned
225 g/8 oz monkfish fillet, skinned
1 tbsp vegetable oil
1 small onion, peeled and chopped
small piece fresh root ginger, peeled
   and grated
2 lemon grass stalks, crushed and
   outer leaves discarded
3 kaffir lime leaves
1 Thai red chilli, deseeded
   and chopped
1 tbsp Thai green curry paste,
   or to taste
1 tbsp light soy sauce
300 ml/$^{1}/_{2}$ pint coconut milk
120 ml/4 fl oz water
2 tbsp lime juice
2 tbsp freshly chopped coriander
freshly cooked fragrant rice, to serve

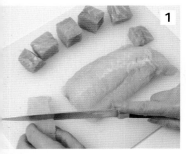

# Aromatic Seafood Curry

1 Cover the saffron strands in cooled boiled water and leave to soak for at least 10 minutes. Prepare the seafood, cleaning the prawns and discarding the thin black vein, if necessary. Scrub the mussels, discarding any that do not close. Rinse the squid and cut into strips, remove the vein from the scallops and cut in half, if large. Cut the fish fillets into small strips. Reserve.

2 Heat the oil in a large saucepan, add the cardamom pods, star anise, garlic, chilli, lemon grass and ginger and gently fry for 1 minute. Stir in the curry paste and cook for 2 minutes.

3 Take off the heat and gradually stir in the coconut milk and water. Bring to the boil, then reduce the heat and simmer for 5 minutes.

4 Add the seafood, starting with the fish pieces, and cook for 2 minutes. Add the prawns, mussels and scallops and cook for a further 3 minutes. Add the squid with the rice wine and cook for 2–3 minutes, or until all the fish is tender. Spoon into a warmed serving dish, sprinkle with the spring onions and serve with fragrant rice.

## Ingredients SERVES 4–6

few saffron strands
450 g/1 lb assorted seafood, such as
    prawns, mussels, squid, scallops
    and white fish fillets
2 tbsp groundnut oil
4 green cardamom pods, cracked
2 whole star anise
3 garlic cloves, peeled and crushed
1 bird's eye chilli, deseeded
    and chopped
2 lemon grass stalks, bruised and
    outer leaves discarded
5 cm/2 inch piece fresh root ginger,
    peeled and grated
1–2 tbsp curry paste, or to taste
300 ml/$^1/_2$ pint coconut milk
150 ml/$^1/_4$ pint water
1 tbsp rice wine
4 spring onions, trimmed and shredded
freshly cooked Thai fragrant rice,
    to serve

## Helpful hint

Dry sherry can be used in place of the rice wine, if preferred.

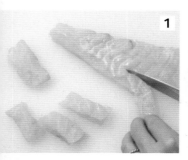

# Thai Coconut Crab Curry

1 Peel the onion and chop finely. Peel the garlic cloves, then either crush or finely chop. Peel the ginger and either grate coarsely or cut into very thin shreds. Reserve.

2 Heat a wok or large frying pan, add the oil and, when hot, add the onion, garlic and ginger and stir-fry for 2 minutes, or until the onion is beginning to soften. Stir in the curry paste and stir-fry for 1 minute.

3 Stir the coconut milk into the vegetable mixture with the dark crab meat. Add the lemon grass, then bring the mixture slowly to the boil, stirring frequently.

4 Add the spring onions and simmer gently for 15 minutes or until the sauce has thickened. Remove and discard the lemon grass stalks.

5 Add the white crab meat and the shredded basil or mint and stir very gently for 1–2 minutes or until heated through and piping hot. Try to prevent the crab meat from breaking up.

6 Spoon the curry over the rice on individual warmed plates, sprinkle with basil or mint leaves and serve immediately.

## Ingredients      SERVES 4–6

1 onion
4 garlic cloves
5 cm/2 inch piece fresh root ginger
2 tbsp vegetable oil
2–3 tsp hot curry paste
400 g/14 oz coconut milk
2 large dressed crabs, white and dark
    meat separated
2 lemon grass stalks, bruised and
    outer leaves discarded
6 spring onions, trimmed
    and chopped
2 tbsp freshly shredded Thai basil or
    mint, plus extra, to garnish
freshly cooked Thai fragrant rice,
    to serve

### Food fact

Lemon grass should be bruised to release its distinctive lemon flavour and scent. This is done by placing it on a chopping board and gently hitting it 2 or 3 times with a rolling pin. For a stronger flavour, finely chop the heart. If it is unavailable, a thin strip of lime or lemon rind makes a good alternative.

# Red Goan Mussels

1 Clean the mussels, removing any beards and discarding any mussels that are open and do not close when tapped lightly on the work surface.

2 Place in a large bowl and cover with cold water, then leave in a cold place, preferably in the refrigerator, until required.

3 Heat the oil in a large saucepan, add the onion, garlic, chillies and celery and fry for 2 minutes. Add the ginger, paprika, turmeric and tamarind and stir well, then gradually stir in the coconut milk and water. Bring to the boil, then reduce the heat and simmer for 5 minutes.

4 Drain the mussels and add to the pan. Cover with a lid and cook for 4–6 minutes, stirring frequently, until the mussels have opened.

5 Spoon into a large serving bowl, such as a soup tureen, and sprinkle with chopped coriander. Serve with warm pitta bread strips.

## Ingredients SERVES 4–6

1 kg/2 lb live mussels
1 tbsp vegetable oil
1 medium onion, peeled and chopped
2–4 garlic cloves, peeled and chopped
1 red chilli, deseeded and chopped
1 green chilli, deseeded and chopped
2 celery sticks, trimmed and thinly sliced
2.5 cm/1 inch piece fresh root ginger, peeled and grated
1 tsp paprika
1 tsp turmeric
2 tsp tamarind paste
300 ml/$^{1}/_{2}$ pint coconut milk
50 ml/2 fl oz water
2 tbsp freshly chopped coriander
warm strips of pitta bread, to serve

### Helpful hint

Discard any mussels that have failed to open during cooking.

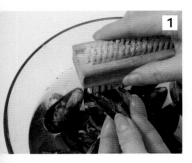

# Creamy Spicy Shellfish

1 Heat a large wok, then add the oil and, when hot, stir-fry the onion and ginger for 2 minutes, or until softened. Add the scallops and stir-fry for 2 minutes, or until the scallops are just cooked. Using a slotted spoon, carefully transfer the scallops to a bowl and keep warm in a low oven.

2 Stir in the garlic, ground cumin, paprika and crushed coriander seeds and cook for 1 minute, stirring constantly. Pour in the lemon juice, sherry and fish stock and bring to the boil. Boil rapidly until reduced by half and slightly thickened.

3 Stir in the cream and return the scallops and any scallop juices to the wok. Bring to the boil and simmer for 1 minute. Add the prawns and mussels and heat through until piping hot. Season to taste with salt and pepper. Sprinkle with freshly chopped coriander and serve immediately with the freshly cooked rice.

## Ingredients                 SERVES 4

2 tbsp groundnut oil
1 onion, peeled and chopped
2.5 cm/1 inch piece fresh root
   ginger, peeled and grated
225 g/8 oz queen scallops, cleaned
   and rinsed
1 garlic clove, peeled and chopped
2 tsp ground cumin
1 tsp paprika
1 tsp coriander seeds, crushed
3 tbsp lemon juice
2 tbsp sherry
300 ml/$^1/_2$ pint fish stock
150 ml/$^1/_4$ pint double cream
225 g/8 oz peeled prawns
225 g/8 oz cooked mussels, shelled
salt and freshly ground black pepper
2 tbsp freshly chopped coriander
freshly cooked rice, to serve

### Helpful hint

Queen scallops are usually bought frozen and tend to have a lot of water in them. Drain them well and absorb excess moisture with kitchen paper to help prevent them shrinking.

# Thai Shellfish Soup

1 Peel the prawns. Using a sharp knife, remove the black vein along the backs of the prawns. Rinse lightly and pat dry with absorbent kitchen paper and reserve.

2 Skin the fish, rinse lightly and pat dry then cut into 2.5 cm/1 inch chunks. Place in a bowl with the prawns and the squid rings. Sprinkle with the lime juice and reserve.

3 Scrub the mussels, removing their beards and any barnacles. Discard any mussels that are open, damaged or that do not close when tapped. Place in a large saucepan and add 150ml/¼ pint of coconut milk. Cover, bring to the boil, then simmer for 5 minutes, or until the mussels open, shaking the saucepan occasionally. Lift out the mussels, discarding any unopened ones, strain the liquid through a muslin-lined sieve and reserve.

4 Rinse and dry the saucepan. Heat the groundnut oil, add the curry paste and cook for 1 minute, stirring all the time. Add the lemon grass, lime leaves and fish sauce and pour in both the strained and the remaining coconut milk. Bring the contents of the saucepan to a very gentle simmer. Add the fish mixture to the saucepan and simmer for 2–3 minutes or until just cooked. Stir in the mussels, with or without their shells as preferred. Season to taste with salt and pepper, then garnish with coriander leaves. Ladle into warmed bowls and serve immediately.

## Ingredients    SERVES 4–6

350 g/12 oz raw prawns
350 g/12 oz firm white fish, such as
    monkfish, cod or haddock
175 g/ 6 oz small squid rings
1 tbsp lime juice
450 g/1 lb live mussels
400 ml/14 fl oz coconut milk
1 tbsp groundnut oil
2 tbsp Thai red curry paste
1 lemon grass stalk, bruised and
    outer leaves discarded
3 kaffir lime leaves, finely shredded
2 tbsp Thai fish sauce
salt and freshly ground black pepper
fresh coriander leaves, to garnish

## Food fact

Sprinkling fish and seafood with lime juice improves its texture, as the acid in the juice firms up the flesh. However, do not leave marinating in the lime juice for too long otherwise the fish will begin to cook.

# Squid in Coconut Sauce

1 Cut the tips off each squid then cut the remainder in half and then into wide strips.

2 Using a small sharp knife, cut a crisscross pattern over both sides. Rinse lightly and reserve.

3 Heat the oil or ghee in a deep frying pan, add the onions and cook gently, stirring frequently, for 5 minutes. Stir in the ginger and garlic purées.

4 Add the cinnamon stick, cloves, cardamom pods, chilli powder, paprika and curry leaves and continue to fry for 2 minutes before stirring in the coconut milk and water. Bring to the boil, then reduce the heat and simmer for 10 minutes.

5 Add the squid and continue to simmer for 4–5 minutes, or until the squid is tender. Sprinkle with the toasted sesame seeds and serve with the freshly cooked rice.

## Ingredients    SERVES 4–6

350 g/12 oz squid, cleaned
1 tbsp vegetable oil or ghee
2 medium onions, peeled
    and chopped
1 tbsp ginger purée
$^1/_2$ tsp garlic purée
1 small cinnamon stick, bruised
2 whole cloves
4 green cardamom pods,
    lightly cracked
1 tsp chilli powder
1 tsp paprika
few curry leaves
300 ml/$^1/_2$ pint coconut milk
85 ml/3 fl oz water
1 tbsp toasted sesame seeds
freshly cooked rice, to serve

## Helpful hint

Take care not to overcook the squid otherwise it will become tough.

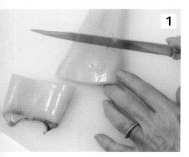

# Vegetables

Meat does not have to feature in your dish to make it a mouthwatering curry. With delicious recipes like Thai Curry with Tofu and Egg & Aubergine Masala, phenomenal vegetable dishes are only pages away. If you are truly looking for a treat for your taste buds, then the exotic Calypso Rice with Curried Bananas is a must-try. Here you will also find some ideal recipes for accompaniments such as Raita.

# Curried Parsnip Soup

1 In a small frying pan, dry-fry the cumin and coriander seeds over a moderately high heat for 1 minute. Shake the pan during cooking until the seeds are lightly toasted. Reserve until cooled. Grind the toasted seeds in a pestle and mortar.

2 Heat the oil in a saucepan. Cook the onion until softened and starting to turn golden. Add the garlic, turmeric, chilli powder and cinnamon stick to the pan. Continue to cook for a further minute.

3 Add the parsnips and stir well. Pour in the stock and bring to the boil. Cover and simmer for 15 minutes or until the parsnips are cooked.

4 Allow the soup to cool. Once cooled, remove the cinnamon stick and discard. Blend the soup in a food processor until very smooth.

5 Transfer to a saucepan and reheat gently. Season to taste with salt and pepper. Garnish with fresh coriander and serve immediately with the yogurt.

## Ingredients SERVES 4

1 tsp cumin seeds
2 tsp coriander seeds
1 tsp oil
1 onion, peeled and chopped
1 garlic clove, peeled and crushed
$1/2$ tsp turmeric
$1/4$ tsp chilli powder
1 cinnamon stick, lightly bruised
450 g/1 lb parsnips, peeled
   and chopped
1 litre/$1^{3}/_{4}$ pint vegetable stock
salt and freshly ground black pepper
fresh coriander leaves,
   to garnish
2–3 tbsp low-fat natural yogurt,
   to serve

## Food fact

Parsnips vary in colour from pale yellow to a creamy white. They are at their best when they are the size of a large carrot. If larger, remove the central core which can be woody.

# Spicy Filled Naan Bread

1 Preheat the oven to 230°C/ 450°F/Gas Mark 8 15 minutes before baking and place a large baking sheet in to heat up. Sift the flour and salt into a large bowl. Stir in the yeast and make a well in the centre. Add the ghee or melted butter, honey and the warm water. Mix to a soft dough.

2 Knead the dough on a lightly floured surface, until smooth and elastic. Put in a lightly oiled bowl, cover with clingfilm and leave to rise for 1 hour, or until doubled in size.

3 For the filling, melt the ghee or butter in a frying pan and gently cook the onion for about 5 minutes. Stir in the garlic and spices and season to taste with salt and pepper. Cook for a further 6–7 minutes, until soft. Remove from the heat, stir in 1 tablespoon of water and leave to cool.

4 Briefly knead the dough, then divide into 6 pieces. Roll out each piece of dough to 12.5 cm/5 inch rounds. Spoon the filling onto one half of each round.

5 Fold over and press the edges together to seal. Re-roll to shape into flat ovals, about 40.5 cm/16 inches long. Cover with oiled clingfilm and leave to rise for about 15 minutes. Transfer the breads to the hot baking sheet and cook in the preheated oven for 10–12 minutes, until puffed up and lightly browned. Serve hot.

## Ingredients    MAKES 6

400 g/14 oz strong white flour
1 tsp salt
1 tsp easy-blend dried yeast
15 g/¹/₂ oz ghee or unsalted
    butter, melted
1 tsp clear honey
200 ml/7 fl oz warm water

### For the filling:

25 g/1 oz ghee or unsalted butter
1 small onion, peeled and
    finely chopped
1 garlic clove, peeled and crushed
1 tsp ground coriander
1 tsp ground cumin
2 tsp grated fresh root ginger
pinch of chilli powder
pinch of ground cinnamon
salt and freshly ground black pepper

### Food fact

Ghee is more expensive than other butters but it has a longer life and a much higher smoke point (190°C/375°F). It is ideal for sautéing and frying.

# Onion Bhajis

1 Finely slice the onions and place in a mixing bowl with the flour, spices and coriander. Add salt to taste.

2 Slowly stir in the water and mix to form a thick consistency. Form into loose balls.

3 Heat the oil in deep-fryer to a temperature of 180°C/350°F. Drop the bhajis, about 2 or 3 at a time, into the hot oil and deep-fry for 2–3 minutes, or until golden brown and crisp. Remove with a slotted spoon and drain on absorbent kitchen paper. Serve.

## Ingredients    SERVES 4–6

2 large onions, peeled
225 g/8 oz chickpea flour
small piece fresh root ginger, peeled and grated
1/2–1 small chilli, deseeded and finely chopped
1/2 tsp turmeric
1/2 tsp ground coriander
4 tbsp freshly chopped coriander
freshly milled salt, to taste
120–150 ml/4–5 fl oz water
vegetable oil, for deep-frying

### Tasty tip

Other ingredients can be used as well – try thinly sliced assorted peppers, courgette, very thinly sliced carrot or even shredded white cabbage.

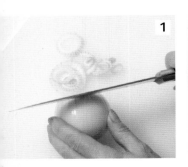

# Vegetable Samosas

**1** Cut the potato into small dice and leave in a bowl of cold water until required. Drain thoroughly and shake dry when ready to use.

**2** Heat 2 tablespoons of the oil in a frying pan, add the mustard seeds and stir-fry for 1 minute, or until they pop. Add the onion and continue to fry for 5–8 minutes, or until softened. Add the remaining oil, if necessary.

**3** Add the spices, chilli and water and cook for a further 3 minutes, then add the potatoes, carrot, peas and beans. Stir, then cover and cook for 10–15 minutes, or until the vegetables are just cooked. Allow to cool.

**4** Cut the pastry into 7.5 cm/3 inch strips. Brush a strip lightly with water and place a second strip on top. Place 1 tablespoon of the filling at one end of the strip then fold the pastry over to form a triangle. Brush the pastry lightly with water. Continue folding the pastry forming triangles to the end of the strip. Repeat with the remaining pastry and filling.

**5** Heat the oil in a deep-fryer to a temperature of 180°C/350°F and deep-fry the samosas, in batches of about 2 or 3 at a time, for 2–3 minutes, or until golden. Remove with a slotted spoon and drain on absorbent kitchen paper. Serve hot or cold.

## Ingredients    SERVES 4–6

150 g/5 oz potatoes, peeled

2–3 tbsp vegetable oil, plus extra for deep-frying

1 tsp mustard seeds

1 onion, peeled and chopped

1 tsp ground coriander

1/2–1 tsp garam masala

1/2 tsp turmeric

1–2 red chillies, deseeded and chopped

2 tbsp water

1 large carrot, peeled and grated

75 g/3 oz frozen peas

75 g/3 oz French beans, trimmed and chopped

250 g/9 oz filo pastry

### Tasty tip

Other ingredients can be used as well – try chickpeas with spinach, onion, chopped red pepper and carrot.

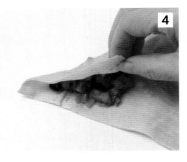

# Sweet Mango Chutney

1 Peel, stone and finely chop the mangos and place in a preserving pan together with the chillies and grated ginger.

2 Add the lemon rind and juice and stir in the water. Bring to the boil, then reduce the heat and simmer for 35–40 minutes, or until the mangos are really soft.

3 Add the sugar and sultanas to the pan and heat gently until the sugar has dissolved. Bring to the boil and continue to boil for 10 minutes, or until a thick consistency is reached. Stir in the balsamic vinegar and cook for a further 5 minutes. Cool slightly then put in clean sterilised jars and seal when cold.

## Ingredients    SERVES 4–6

4 ripe mangos, about 900 g/2 lb
   in weight
1–2 red chillies, deseeded
   and chopped
5 cm/2 inch piece fresh root ginger,
   peeled and grated
grated rind and juice 3 lemons,
   preferably unwaxed (organic)
600 ml/1 pint water
450 g/1 lb light muscovado sugar
175 g/6 oz golden sultanas
2–3 tbsp balsamic vinegar

## Tasty tip

Other flavours can be used, if liked – try adding 2 vanilla pods, or 4 star anise, 6 lightly cracked cardamom pods and 2 whole cloves, tied in a small piece of muslin.

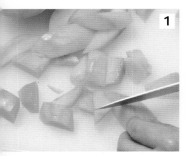

# Tomato & Onion Raita

1 Grate the ginger on the coarse grater or finely chop and place in a small mixing bowl together with the chillies and onion.

2 Discard the seeds from the cucumber and finely chop the flesh, then add to the bowl. Deseed the tomatoes, finely chop the flesh and add to the bowl.

3 Stir in the yogurt and coriander. Mix well, cover lightly and store in the refrigerator until required.

**Ingredients**   SERVES 4–6

small piece fresh root ginger, peeled
2 mild green chillies, deseeded and
   finely chopped
1 onion, peeled and finely chopped
5 cm/2 inch piece cucumber, peeled
2 ripe tomatoes
200 ml/7 fl oz natural yogurt
1 tbsp freshly chopped coriander

# Mint Raita

1 Mix all the ingredients together and spoon into a serving bowl. Cover lightly and store in the refrigerator until required. Leave for at least 30 minutes to allow the flavours to develop.

**Food fact**

Chillies vary in heat and a rough guide to gauge the heat is often: 'the smaller the chilli, the hotter it is'. They are also graded by number with number 1 being very mild and number 10 extremely hot.

**Ingredients**   SERVES 4–6

5 cm/2 inch piece cucumber,
   deseeded and finely chopped
6 spring onions, trimmed and
   finely chopped
2–3 garlic cloves, peeled and crushed
200 ml/7 fl oz natural yogurt
freshly milled salt and freshly ground
   black pepper
3 tbsp freshly chopped mint

# Thai-style Cauliflower & Potato Curry

1 Bring a saucepan of lightly salted water to the boil, add the potatoes and cook for 15 minutes or until just tender. Drain and leave to cool. Boil the cauliflower for 2 minutes, then drain and refresh under cold running water. Drain again and reserve.

2 Meanwhile, blend the garlic, onion, ground almonds and spices with 2 tablespoons of the oil, and salt and pepper to taste in a food processor until a smooth paste is formed. Heat a wok, add the remaining oil and, when hot, add the spice paste and cook for 3–4 minutes, stirring continuously.

3 Dissolve the creamed coconut in 6 tablespoons of boiling water and add to the wok. Pour in the stock, cook for 2–3 minutes, then stir in the cooked potatoes and cauliflower.

4 Stir in the mango chutney and heat through for 3–4 minutes or until piping hot. Tip into a warmed serving dish, garnish with sprigs of fresh coriander and serve immediately with freshly cooked rice.

## Ingredients          SERVES 4

450 g/1 lb new potatoes, peeled and
   halved or quartered
350 g/12 oz cauliflower florets
3 garlic cloves, peeled and crushed
1 onion, peeled and finely chopped
40 g/1$\frac{1}{2}$ oz ground almonds
1 tsp ground coriander
$\frac{1}{2}$ tsp ground cumin
$\frac{1}{2}$ tsp turmeric
3 tbsp groundnut oil
salt and freshly ground black pepper
50 g/2 oz creamed coconut, broken
   into small pieces
200 ml/7 fl oz vegetable stock
1 tbsp mango chutney
sprigs of fresh coriander, to garnish
freshly cooked long-grain rice,
   to serve

## Helpful hint

Mildly flavoured vegetables absorb the taste and colour of spices in this dish. Do not overcook the cauliflower; it should be only just tender for this dish. Broccoli florets could be used instead.

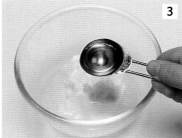

# Curried Potatoes with Spinach

1 Cut the potatoes into small cubes and reserve. Dry-fry the cumin seeds in a saucepan for 30 seconds, then add the oil and potatoes and cook for 3–5 minutes, stirring, or until the potatoes are beginning to turn golden.

2 Add the onion, garlic and chilli and continue to cook for 2–3 minutes, or until the onion is beginning to soften. Sprinkle in the ground coriander and turmeric and cook for a further 2 minutes.

3 Chop the tomatoes and stir into the pan. Cover and cook, stirring occasionally, for 10 minutes, or until the potatoes are tender. Stir in the spinach, water and seasoning, to taste, and cook for 2 minutes, or until the spinach has wilted, then serve.

## Ingredients SERVES 4–6

300 g/10 oz potatoes, peeled
1 tsp cumin seeds
2 tbsp vegetable oil
1 onion, peeled and chopped
2 garlic cloves, peeled and crushed
1 red chilli, deseeded and
  finely chopped
1 tsp ground coriander
$1/2$ tsp turmeric
4 tomatoes
450 g/1 lb fresh leaf spinach, lightly
  rinsed and chopped
50 ml/2 fl oz water
salt and freshly ground black pepper

**Tasty tip:**
This is an ideal accompaniment for all curries as well as being a good snack for lunch or supper.

# Thai Curry with Tofu

1   Pour 450 ml/³⁄₄ pint of the coconut milk into a saucepan and bring to the boil. Add the tofu, season to taste with salt and pepper and simmer gently for 10 minutes. Using a slotted spoon, remove the tofu and place on a plate. Reserve the coconut milk.

2   Place the garlic, onion, dried chillies, lemon rind, ginger, spices and soy sauce in a blender or food processor and blend until a smooth paste is formed. Pour the remaining 150 ml/¹⁄₄ pint coconut milk into a clean saucepan and whisk in the spicy paste. Cook, stirring continuously, for 15 minutes.

3   Gradually whisk the reserved coconut milk into the curry and heat to simmering point. Add the cooked tofu and cook for 5–10 minutes. Blend the cornflour with 1 tablespoon of cold water and stir into the curry. Cook until thickened. Turn into a warmed serving dish and garnish with chilli, lemon wedges and coriander. Serve immediately with Thai fragrant rice.

## Ingredients          SERVES 4

600 ml/1 pint coconut milk
250 g/9 oz firm tofu, drained and cut
    into small cubes
salt and freshly ground black pepper
4 garlic cloves, peeled and chopped
1 large onion, peeled and cut
    into wedges
1 tsp crushed dried chillies
grated rind 1 lemon
2.5 cm/1 inch piece fresh root
    ginger, peeled and grated
1 tbsp ground coriander
1 tsp ground cumin
1 tsp turmeric
2 tbsp light soy sauce
1 tsp cornflour
Thai fragrant rice, to serve

### To garnish:

2 red chillies, deseeded and cut
    into rings
1 tbsp freshly chopped coriander
lemon wedges

# Vegetable Kofta Curry

1 Bring a saucepan of lightly salted water to the boil. Add the potatoes, carrots and parsnips. Cover and simmer for 12–15 minutes, or until the vegetables are tender. Drain the vegetables and mash until very smooth. Stir the egg into the vegetable purée, then add the flour and mix to make a stiff paste and reserve.

2 Heat 2 tablespoons of the oil in a wok and gently cook the onions for 10 minutes. Add the garlic and ginger and cook for a further 2–3 minutes, or until very soft and just beginning to colour.

3 Sprinkle the garam masala over the onions and stir in. Add the tomato paste and stock. Bring to the boil, cover and simmer gently for 15 minutes.

4 Meanwhile, heat the remaining oil in a wok or frying pan. Drop in tablespoons of vegetable batter, 4 or 5 at a time, and fry, turning often, for 3-4 minutes until brown and crisp. Remove with a slotted spoon and drain on absorbent kitchen paper. Keep warm in a low oven while cooking the rest.

5 Stir the yogurt and coriander into the onion sauce. Slowly heat to boiling point and season to taste with salt and pepper. Divide the koftas between warmed serving plates and spoon over the sauce. Serve immediately.

## Ingredients     SERVES 6

350 g/12 oz potatoes, peeled and diced
225 g/8 oz carrots, peeled and roughly chopped
225 g/8 oz parsnips, peeled and roughly chopped
1 egg, lightly beaten
75 g/3 oz plain flour, sifted
8 tbsp vegetable oil
2 onions, peeled and sliced
2 garlic cloves, peeled and crushed
2.5 cm/1 inch piece fresh root ginger, peeled and grated
$1/2$–1 tbsp garam masala
2 tbsp tomato paste
300 ml/$1/2$ pint vegetable stock
250 ml/8 fl oz Greek style yogurt
3 tbsp freshly chopped coriander
salt and freshly ground black pepper

## Food fact

Greek yogurt is made by straining the excess watery liquid from ordinary yogurt, making it thicker and higher in fat than natural yogurt.

# Pumpkin & Chickpea Curry

1 Heat 1 tablespoon of the oil in a saucepan and add the onion. Fry gently for 5 minutes until softened.

2 Add the garlic, ginger and spices and fry for a further minute. Add the chopped tomatoes and chillies and cook for another minute.

3 Add the pumpkin and curry paste and fry gently for 3–4 minutes before adding the stock. Stir well, bring to the boil and simmer for 20 minutes until the pumpkin is tender.

4 Thickly slice the banana and add to the pumpkin along with the chickpeas. Simmer for a further 5 minutes.

5 Season to taste with salt and pepper and add the chopped coriander. Serve immediately, garnished with coriander sprigs and some rice or naan bread.

## Ingredients SERVES 4

1 tbsp vegetable oil
1 small onion, peeled and sliced
2 garlic cloves, peeled and finely chopped
2.5 cm/1 inch piece root ginger, peeled and grated
1 tsp ground coriander
$^1/_2$ tsp ground cumin
$^1/_2$ tsp ground turmeric
$^1/_4$ tsp ground cinnamon
2 tomatoes, chopped
2 red bird's eye chillies, deseeded and finely chopped
450 g/1 lb pumpkin or butternut squash flesh, cubed
1 tbsp hot curry paste
300 ml/$^1/_2$ pint vegetable stock
1 large firm banana
400 g/14 oz can chickpeas, drained and rinsed
salt and freshly ground black pepper
1 tbsp freshly chopped coriander
coriander sprigs, to garnish
rice or naan bread, to serve

# Creamy Chickpea Curry

1 Heat the oil in a frying pan, add the cinnamon stick, cardamom pods, fennel seeds and ginger and cook gently for 3 minutes, stirring frequently. Add the garlic, chillies, onion and remaining spices to the pan and cook gently, stirring occasionally, for 3–5 minutes, or until the onion has softened.

2 Add the chickpeas and water. Bring to the boil, then reduce the heat and simmer for 15 minutes.

3 Blend the tomato purée with a little of the coconut milk then add to the chickpeas with the remaining coconut milk and tomatoes. Cook for 8–10 minutes, or until the tomatoes have begun to collapse. Stir in the chopped coriander and serve.

## Ingredients SERVES 4–6

2 tbsp vegetable oil

1 cinnamon stick, bruised

3 cardamom pods, bruised

1 tsp fennel seeds

5 cm/2 inch piece fresh root ginger, peeled and grated

2 garlic cloves, peeled and crushed

2 red chillies, deseeded and chopped

1 large onion, peeled and chopped

1 tsp ground fenugreek

1 tsp garam masala

$^1/_2$ tsp turmeric

2 x 400 g/14 oz cans chickpeas, drained and rinsed

300 ml/$^1/_2$ pint water

1 tsp tomato purée

300 ml/$^1/_2$ pint coconut milk

225 g/8 oz cherry tomatoes, halved

2 tbsp freshly chopped coriander

## Helpful hint

Medium-sized tomatoes can be used, if preferred – simply chop rather than halve and use as above.

# Mung Bean Curry

1 Break the coconut into small pieces and place in a food processor or liquidiser with one of the chillies and 3 tablespoons of water. Blend for 1 minute, then, with the motor still running, gradually pour in the remaining water to form a thin smooth liquid. Reserve.

2 Place the mung beans, remaining chilli and turmeric in a saucepan and cover with water. Bring to the boil, then reduce the heat and simmer for 20 minutes. Cut the potatoes into small chunks and add to the saucepan together with the onion and French beans. Continue to cook for 8 minutes.

3 Pour in the coconut liquid and cook, stirring occasionally, for a further 10 minutes, or until the beans and vegetables are tender.

4 Meanwhile, heat the oil in a small frying pan, add the mustard seeds and the curry leaves and fry for 1 minute, or until the mustard seeds pop. Stir well then stir into the curry. Serve.

## Ingredients    SERVES 4–6

50 g/2 oz creamed coconut
2 red chillies, deseeded and
   finely chopped
250 ml/8 fl oz water
250 g/9 oz canned mung beans
$1/2$ tsp turmeric
225 g/8 oz potatoes, peeled
1 onion, peeled and cut into wedges
175 g/6 oz French beans, trimmed
   and chopped
2 tbsp vegetable oil
1 tsp brown mustard seeds
5–6 curry leaves

### Helpful hint

If you cannot find canned mung beans, then use dried ones. You will need to soak them overnight before cooking. After soaking, rinse then boil rapidly for 10 minutes, before reducing the heat and simmering for about 20 minutes or until tender.

# Spinach Dhal

1 Rinse the lentils and place in a saucepan with the onions, potato, chilli, water and turmeric. Bring to the boil, then reduce the heat, cover and simmer for 15 minutes, or until the lentils are tender and most of the liquid has been absorbed.

2 Chop the spinach and add to the pan with the tomatoes and cook for a further 5 minutes, or until the spinach has wilted.

3 Heat the oil in a frying pan, add the mustard seeds and fry for 1 minute, or until they pop. Add the curry leaves, stir well then stir into the dhal and serve.

## Ingredients     SERVES 4–6

100 g/4 oz split red lentils

2 onions, peeled and chopped

225 g/8 oz potato, peeled and cut
    into small chunks

1 green chilli, deseeded and chopped

150 ml/$^1/_4$ pint water

1 tsp turmeric

175 g/6 oz fresh spinach

2 tomatoes, chopped

2 tbsp vegetable oil

1 tsp mustard seeds

few curry leaves

## Helpful hint

It is important that spices are stored correctly otherwise their flavour can be impaired. Unless you use a lot of spice, buy in small quantities and store in a cool dark place. If you have time, grind your own spice powders to give a greater and more flavourful aroma and taste.

# Tarka Dhal

1    Deseed the chillies and chop. Rinse the lentils then place in a large saucepan with the onions, 2 of the sliced garlic cloves, the chillies, tomatoes, turmeric and water. Bring to the boil, then reduce the heat, cover and simmer for 20 minutes. Remove the lid and cook for a further 5 minutes.

2    Heat the oil in a frying pan, add the seeds and remaining sliced garlic and cook for 1–2 minutes, or until lightly browned.

3    Place the cooked lentil mixture into a warmed serving bowl, stir in the chopped coriander and sprinkle the toasted seeds and garlic on top. Serve.

## Ingredients    SERVES 4–6

2 green chillies
200 g/7 oz red split lentils
175 g/6 oz yellow split lentils
2 onions, peeled and chopped
4 garlic cloves, peeled and sliced
2 tomatoes, chopped
1 tsp turmeric
1.2 litres/2 pints water
2 tbsp vegetable oil
1 tsp cumin seeds
1 tsp fennel seeds
2 tbsp freshly chopped coriander

## Food fact

Dhal is a thick soup-like dish and nearly always contains lentils and usually another pulse as well. It is eaten by many people and forms an integral part of the meal.

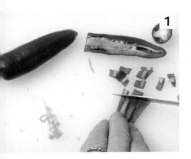

# Paneer & Pea Curry

1 Cut the paneer into small cubes. Heat the oil in a deep fryer to a temperature of 180°C/350°F then deep-fry the paneer cubes for 3–4 minutes, or until golden brown. Drain on absorbent kitchen paper and reserve.

2 Heat the 2 tablespoons of oil in a frying pan, add the seeds and fry for 1–2 minutes, or until they pop. Add the onions, garlic and chillies and continue to fry for 5 minutes, stirring frequently, until slightly softened. Sprinkle in the turmeric, fenugreek and garam masala and cook for a further 5 minutes.

3 Stir in the chopped tomatoes and sugar snap peas and continue to cook for 10 minutes, or until the peas are tender. Stir in a little water if the mixture is getting too dry. Add the fried paneer and heat for 2–3 minutes before stirring in the cream. Heat gently for 2–3 minutes, then stir in the chopped coriander. Serve.

## Ingredients       SERVES 4–6

225 g/8 oz paneer
vegetable oil, for deep-frying, plus 2
    tbsp for shallow-frying
1½ tsp cumin seeds
1½ tsp fennel seeds
3 onions, peeled and chopped
3 garlic cloves, peeled and chopped
1–2 red chillies, deseeded
    and chopped
1½ tsp turmeric
1½ tsp ground fenugreek
1½ tsp garam masala
4 tomatoes, chopped
300 g/10 oz sugar snap peas
50 ml/2 fl oz water (optional)
4 tbsp double cream
2 tbsp freshly chopped coriander

### Food fact

Paneer cheese is perhaps India's most well-known cheese. It has a firm texture and works well when fried, grilled or pan-fried.

# Creamy Vegetable Korma

1 Heat the ghee or oil in a large saucepan. Add the onion and cook for 5 minutes. Stir in the garlic and ginger and cook for a further 5 minutes, or until soft and just beginning to colour.

2 Stir in the cracked cardamom pods, ground coriander, cumin and turmeric. Continue cooking over a low heat for 1 minute, stirring.

3 Stir in the lemon rind and juice and almonds. Blend in the vegetable stock. Slowly bring to the boil, stirring occasionally.

4 Add the potatoes and vegetables. Bring back to the boil, then reduce the heat, cover and simmer for 35–40 minutes, or until the vegetables are just tender. Check after 25 minutes and add a little more stock if needed.

5 Slowly stir in the cream and chopped coriander. Season to taste with salt and pepper. Cook very gently until heated through, but do not boil. Discard the cardamom pods and serve immediately with naan bread.

## Ingredients    SERVES 4–6

2 tbsp ghee or vegetable oil
1 large onion, peeled and chopped
2 garlic cloves, peeled and crushed
2.5 cm/1 inch piece root ginger,
    peeled and grated
4 cardamom pods, cracked
2 tsp ground coriander
1 tsp ground cumin
1 tsp ground turmeric
finely grated rind and juice
    $^1/_2$ lemon
50 g/2 oz ground almonds
400 ml/14 fl oz vegetable stock
450 g/1 lb potatoes, peeled and diced
450 g/1 lb mixed vegetables, such as
    cauliflower, carrots and turnip, cut
    into chunks
150 ml/$^1/_4$ pint double cream
3 tbsp freshly chopped coriander
salt and freshly ground black pepper
naan bread, to serve

# Calypso Rice with Curried Bananas

1 Heat the oil in a large frying pan and gently cook the onion for 10 minutes until soft. Add the garlic, chilli and red pepper and cook for 2–3 minutes. Rinse the rice under cold running water, then add to the pan and stir. Pour in the lime juice and stock, bring to the boil, cover and simmer for 12–15 minutes, or until the rice is tender and the stock is absorbed.

2 Stir in the black-eye beans and chopped parsley and season to taste with salt and pepper. Leave to stand, covered, for 5 minutes before serving, to allow the beans to warm through.

3 While the rice is cooking, make the Curried Bananas. Remove the skins from the bananas – they may need to be cut off with a sharp knife. Slice the flesh thickly. Heat the oil in a frying pan and cook the bananas, in 2 batches, for 2–3 minutes, or until lightly browned.

4 Pour the coconut milk into the pan and stir in the curry paste. Add the banana slices to the coconut milk and simmer, uncovered, over a low heat for 8–10 minutes, or until the bananas are very soft and the coconut milk slightly reduced.

5 Spoon the rice onto warmed serving plates, garnish with coriander and serve immediately with the Curried Bananas.

## Ingredients SERVES 4

2 tbsp vegetable oil
1 onion, peeled and finely chopped
1 garlic clove, peeled and crushed
1 red chilli, deseeded and finely chopped
1 red pepper, deseeded and chopped
225 g/8 oz basmati rice
juice of 1 lime
350 ml/12 fl oz vegetable stock
200 g can black-eye beans, drained
    and rinsed
2 tbsp freshly chopped parsley
salt and freshly ground black pepper
sprigs of coriander, to garnish

### For the curried bananas:

4 green bananas
2 tbsp vegetable oil
200 ml/7 fl oz coconut milk
2 tsp mild curry paste

### Food fact

Another name for green bananas is plantains. They should not be eaten raw and used in savoury dishes only.

# Vegetable Biryani

1 Preheat the oven to 200°C/400°F/Gas Mark 6. Put 1 tablespoon of the vegetable oil in a large bowl with the onions and toss to coat. Lightly brush or spray a nonstick baking sheet with a little more oil. Spread half the onions on the baking sheet and cook at the top of the preheated oven for 15–20 minutes, stirring regularly, until golden and crisp. Remove from the oven and reserve for the garnish.

2 Meanwhile, heat a large ovenproof casserole over a medium heat and add the remaining oil and onions. Cook for 5–7 minutes until softened and starting to brown. Add a little water if they start to stick. Add the garlic and ginger and cook for another minute, then add the carrot, parsnip and sweet potato. Cook the vegetables for a further 5 minutes. Add the curry paste and stir for a minute until everything is coated, then stir in the rice and tomatoes. After 2 minutes, add the stock and stir well. Bring to the boil, cover and simmer over a very gentle heat for about 10 minutes.

3 Add the cauliflower and peas and cook for 8–10 minutes, or until the rice is tender. Season to taste with salt and pepper. Serve garnished with the crispy onions, cashew nuts, raisins and coriander. To alleviate the dryness, biryani is best served with dhal and raita.

## Ingredients          SERVES 4

2 tbsp vegetable oil, plus a little extra
   for brushing
2 large onions, peeled and thinly
   sliced lengthways
2 garlic cloves, peeled and
   finely chopped
2.5 cm/1 inch piece fresh root
   ginger, peeled and finely grated
1 small carrot, peeled and cut into sticks
1 small parsnip, peeled and diced
1 small sweet potato, peeled and diced
1 tbsp medium curry paste
225 g/8 oz basmati rice
4 ripe tomatoes, peeled, deseeded
   and diced
600 ml/1 pint vegetable stock
175 g/6 oz cauliflower florets
50 g/2 oz peas, thawed if frozen
salt and freshly ground black pepper

### To garnish:

Crispy onion rings; freshly ground
black pepper; roasted cashew nuts;
raisins and fresh coriander leaves.

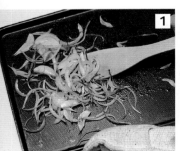

# Egg & Aubergine Curry

1 Place the eggs in a saucepan and cover with cold water. Bring to the boil and continue to boil for 10 minutes. Drain and plunge into cold water and leave until cold. Drain, shell and reserve.

2 Heat the oil in a saucepan, add the cumin seeds and fry for 30 seconds, or until they pop. Add the onions, garlic, chillies and ginger and cook for 5 minutes, or until the onion has softened. Add the spices and continue to cook for a further 5 minutes.

3 Halve the baby aubergines and add to the pan with the chopped tomatoes then simmer gently, stirring occasionally, for 12–15 minutes, or until the aubergine is tender. Stir in the cream and cook for a further 3 minutes. Cut the eggs into quarters, add to the pan and stir gently. Heat for 2 minutes before sprinkling with chopped coriander and serving.

## Ingredients    SERVES 4–6

4 eggs
2 tbsp vegetable oil
1 tsp cumin seeds
2 onions, peeled and chopped
2–3 garlic cloves, deseeded and
    finely chopped
2 green chillies, deseeded and
    finely chopped
5 cm/2 inch piece fresh root ginger,
    peeled and grated
1 tsp turmeric
1 tsp ground coriander
1 tsp garam masala
450 g/1 lb baby aubergines, trimmed
400 g/14 oz can chopped tomatoes
4 tbsp double cream
2 tbsp freshly chopped coriander

### Helpful hint

If baby aubergines are not available use large aubergines cut into chunks instead.

# Sweet Potato Curry

1 Heat the oil in a sauté pan or wok, add the chillies, ginger and spices and fry for 3 minutes, stirring frequently. Add the onions and garlic and continue to fry for a further 5 minutes, or until the onion has softened.

2 Add the sweet potatoes and stir until coated in the spices, then add the green pepper and chopped tomatoes.

3 Pour in the coconut milk. Bring to the boil, then reduce the heat, cover and simmer for 12–15 minutes, or until the vegetables are cooked. Stir in the spinach and heat for 3 minutes, or until wilted. Add the curry leaves, stir and serve.

## Ingredients    SERVES 4–6

2 tbsp vegetable oil
2 green chillies, deseeded and chopped
5 cm/2 inch piece fresh root ginger, peeled and grated
$\frac{1}{2}$–1 tsp chilli powder
1 tsp turmeric
1 tsp ground cumin
1 tsp ground coriander
2 onions, peeled and cut into wedges
2–3 garlic cloves, peeled and crushed
450 g/1 lb sweet potatoes, peeled and cut into small chunks
1 large green pepper, deseeded and chopped
4 tomatoes, chopped
300 ml/$\frac{1}{2}$ pint coconut milk
225 g/8 oz fresh spinach leaves
few curry leaves

## Helpful hint

As curry leaves are not that easy to find it is worth buying a good number then wrapping them well in freezer wrap and freezing.

# Mixed Vegetable Curry

**1** Heat the oil in a large saucepan or wok, add the seeds and fry for 30 seconds, or until they pop.

**2** Add the garlic, curry powder and onions and cook gently for 5 minutes, or until the onions have softened.

**3** Add the remaining vegetables, except for the peas and tomatoes, to the pan. Add the water, bring to the boil, then reduce the heat, cover and simmer for 15 minutes.

**4** Add the peas and tomatoes and continue to simmer for a further 5 minutes. Stir in the curry leaves, ground almonds and yogurt. Heat gently for 3 minutes, or until hot. Garnish with chopped coriander and serve.

## Ingredients    SERVES 4–6

2 tbsp vegetable oil

1 tsp cumin seeds

1 tsp black mustard seeds

2–3 garlic cloves, peeled and chopped

1 tbsp hot curry powder

2 onions, peeled and cut into wedges

225 g/8 oz sweet potatoes, peeled and chopped

225 g/8 oz potatoes, peeled and chopped

175 g/6 oz carrots, peeled and chopped

175 g/6 oz cauliflower, cut into small florets

300 ml/$^1/_2$ pint water

100 g/4 oz frozen peas

3 tomatoes, chopped

few fresh curry leaves, chopped

2 tbsp ground almonds

4 tbsp natural yogurt

1 tbsp freshly chopped coriander, to garnish

### Tasty tip

For more substance, add a drained and rinsed 400 g/14 oz can of chickpeas.

# Vegetable & Coconut Stew

1    Heat the oil or ghee in a large saucepan, add the seeds, cinnamon stick, cloves, cardamom pods and chilli powder and fry for 30 seconds, or until the seeds pop.

2    Add the shallots, garlic, potatoes, squash and carrots and stir until the vegetables are coated in the flavoured oil. Add the water, bring to the boil, then reduce the heat, cover and simmer for 15 minutes.

3    Pour in the coconut milk and add the chopped beans and kidney beans. Stir well then cook for a further 10 minutes. Sprinkle with the chopped spring onions and serve.

## Ingredients    SERVES 4–6

2 tbsp vegetable oil or ghee

1 tsp cumin seeds

1 cinnamon stick, bruised

3 whole cloves

3 cardamom pods, bruised

½–1 tsp chilli powder

8 shallots, peeled and halved

2–3 garlic cloves, peeled and finely chopped

225 g/8 oz potatoes, peeled and cut into chunks

½ butternut squash, about 350 g/12 oz in weight, peeled, deseeded and cut into chunks

225 g/8 oz carrots, peeled and chopped

200 ml/7 fl oz water

300 ml/½ pint coconut milk

225 g/8 oz French beans, trimmed and chopped

400 g/14 oz can red kidney beans, drained and rinsed

4–6 spring onions, trimmed and finely chopped

# Pumpkin Curry

1 Dry-fry the desiccated coconut in a nonstick frying pan, stirring constantly, for 2 minutes, or until lightly toasted. Remove and reserve.

2 Heat the oil or ghee in a large saucepan, add all the seeds and cook, stirring, for 30 seconds, or until they pop. Add the ground spices and stir well before adding the chillies, onions and garlic. Cook for 5 minutes, stirring frequently.

3 Add the pumpkin and stir until lightly coated in the spices, then stir in the red pepper, tomatoes and water. Bring to the boil, reduce the heat, cover and simmer for 15–20 minutes, or until the pumpkin is tender. Sprinkle with the toasted coconut and serve.

## Ingredients                SERVES 4–6

25 g/1 oz desiccated coconut (or grated fresh coconut)
2 tbsp vegetable oil or ghee
1 tsp black mustard seeds
1 tsp fennel seeds
1 tsp cracked cumin seeds
1 tsp ground fenugreek
1 tsp ground cinnamon
1 tsp turmeric
1–2 red chillies, deseeded and chopped
2 onions, peeled and chopped
3 garlic cloves, peeled and chopped
450 g/1 lb pumpkin, peeled, deseeded and cut into small chunks
1 large red pepper, deseeded and chopped
225 g/8 oz ripe tomatoes, chopped
150 ml/$^1/_4$ pint water

# Okra Moru Curry

1 Heat the oil in a heavy-based saucepan, add the chillies and ginger and cook for 2 minutes, stirring frequently. Using a slotted spoon, remove half of the mixture and reserve.

2 Add the garlic, onions and ground cumin and coriander and cook for a further 5 minutes, stirring frequently. Add the okra and cook, stirring, until the okra is lightly coated in the spices and oil.

3 Add the chopped tomatoes with their juice, then bring to the boil, reduce the heat, cover and simmer for 12–15 minutes, or until the okra is tender.

4 Meanwhile, blend the reserved chilli mixture with the yogurt and turmeric. Pour into a small saucepan and heat gently for 3 minutes. Pour over the okra and serve.

## Ingredients     SERVES 4–6

2 tbsp vegetable oil
2 red chillies, deseeded and chopped
1 green chilli, deseeded and chopped
5 cm/2 inch piece fresh root
    ginger, grated
2–3 garlic cloves, peeled and crushed
2 onions, peeled and cut into
    small wedges
1 tsp ground cumin
1 tsp ground coriander
450 g/1 lb okra, trimmed and sliced,
    if large
400 g/14 oz can chopped tomatoes
150 ml/¼ pint natural yogurt
½–1 tsp turmeric

### Helpful hint

If the piece of root ginger is fresh, it is not strictly necessary to peel before grating. It is a case of personal choice.

# Mixed Pepper Moru Curry

1. Heat the 2 tablespoons of oil or ghee in a heavy-based frying pan, add the seeds and fry for 30 seconds, or until they pop. Add the fenugreek, garlic and onions and cook, stirring occasionally, for 5 minutes, or until the onions have softened.

2. Add the pepper strips and beans to the pan, stir well and add the chopped tomatoes and water. Bring to the boil, then reduce the heat, cover and simmer for 12–15 minutes, or until the vegetables are tender. Spoon into a serving dish.

3. Meanwhile, heat the 2 teaspoons of oil or ghee in a frying pan, add the ginger and chillies and cook for 2 minutes. Stir in the turmeric, then slowly stir in the yogurt. Heat, stirring, until blended and hot. Pour over the peppers and serve.

## Ingredients    SERVES 4–6

2 tbsp vegetable oil or ghee, plus 2 tsp

1 tsp cumin seeds

1 tsp poppy seeds

1 tsp fennel seeds

1 tsp ground fenugreek

3 garlic cloves, peeled and chopped

2 red onions, peeled and chopped

6 assorted peppers, deseeded and cut into strips

225 g/8 oz French beans, trimmed and chopped

4 ripe tomatoes, chopped

3 tbsp water

2.5 cm/1 inch piece fresh root ginger, peeled and grated

2 green chillies, deseeded and chopped

1 tsp turmeric

150 ml/$^1/_4$ pint natural yogurt

## Food fact

Moru curries are finished with a thin yellow sauce made from yogurt, chillies, ginger and turmeric, which is stirred in at the end of the cooking time.

# Index